Oh... So Now You Think You're Grown?!

SELF ENHANCEMENT BOOK FOR A GIRL WHO'S ON HER JOURNEY TO WOMANHOOD

SHANELLE SARA'NITA

A LIGHT OF RAE PRODUCTION

Book cover design and interior layout by Olivia Heyward | OH Creative Boutique

ISBN 9780578662664

First printing edition 2020

Acknowledgments

Well, God! You've done it again! You've allowed me to go through the storms and shine bright through the clouds. Life, thus far, has been a journey; and I am forever grateful for every bump in the road, every memory, and every mountain that gave me the ability to show myself, and this world, my truth and my resilience. Thank you. This book is dedicated to a few people who have had positive impacts on my life, and of course a few negatives; but we will get to that later.

Chloe'Rae Monroe and Harley Sienna'Lynn - my two beautiful, most amazing daughters…I am forever grateful and honored to say I am your mother. I must admit, motherhood was scary for me; but I have not received a better gift than the love you two give to me. You are my strength, my life coaches, my Heaven on Earth, and I could not breathe a day without your smiles. This book is dedicated to you. I vow to protect you, love you, and give you the tools to be amazing women and leaders. Put God first in everything you do, because my guidance will not be enough. I pray that our bond grows closer every day, and I hope that I am making you two proud. I love you, my Tink and Toots.

Husband! I say that word with pride and joy. We are not perfect, but we have stood through the test of time, trials, and tribulations. There is no better person to stand behind. You are so much more than just a conqueror. I thank God for you and our children every day. I pray that your strength grows stronger than ever, and that you receive all that God has for you. Who would have known that exchanging numbers in Social Studies class would have turned into a lifetime? I look forward to taking on this world with you. I love you, Anthony Ladd.

Mommy! I would not have the confidence or the courage to do any of the things I've done in my life if it wasn't for you. You planted a seed in me that has kept me going for so long. Mommy… I love you!

Ronald and Erykah - You two have no idea how much I love you. I may not have made all of the best choices, but I pray that as your sister, I have been a great example to you. I am proud of the both of you.

My dear Sister-Cousin, Deidre Percal Samantha Baker. This will be the hardest part of writing this book, but if I didn't acknowledge the fight in you I would not be doing any of us justice. You are my Hero. You spent your entire twenties fighting one illness after another with a smile on your face. You taught me to not take life for granted and to smile even when things don't look good. Our childhood memories are filled with laughing until our stomachs hurt, and dancing to "Independent Women" in the living room after a long day at work. Just know that I miss you so much, I can't stand it. I love you, and I thank you for bringing that beautiful smile into my life; for loving my daughter like she is your own, and for teaching me to not judge a person by their way of life, but to love them unconditionally. Watch over us and flap those golden wings!

Daddy, the majority of this book is written from your love, experience, and lectures. You have planted a seed in me that has blossomed and become a legacy. There is so much that I've learned from you. You are no longer here in the physical, but I will continue to speak your name and carry on your words of wisdom. I will remember your laughter and those "I told you so" moments. I love you!

Roberta "Mama" and Grandma Lauretta. I love you so much! Mama, our daily conversations have gotten me through so many days. I have become a woman of God because of what you have poured into me. Grandma Lauretta, I know you don't think much of this world, and you have lost so much, but I am so thankful for you and the beauty you possess.

I want to acknowledge my apostles Gregory and Junie Kelley of Restoration of Life through Jesus Christ in Jonesboro, Ga. I was welcomed in with open arms, and my experience has been filled with joy. I thank you for helping to mold me into a better woman. I've never felt so at home in my life. Thank you for taking time to counsel me and teach me. For listening to my problems and helping us through hard times and setting me straight when I needed to be. I am forever grateful for you both.

I want to acknowledge the young women in my family. I was literally about to write each one of you down in this book until I realized how long it would take. Even though I may not see some of you often, please know that each one of you were on my mind while writing this book. And, I mean each one of you (this is probably why I should've mentioned your names, because you'll think I am lying). All of you have inspired me in one way or another

Last, but not least, I want to thank you. Yes, **YOU!** The girl that's reading this book. Girl, we are about to go on a journey together, and I am proud to be a part of it. You have inspired me to share my life and experiences. So, I want to thank you! Not just for supporting me, but for trusting me with your mind and heart. I wrote this book because I believe that WE are the greatest assets to this world. I pray that you take this book and use it as a tool for the rest of your life. Share it with another girl, and another, and another. Let's mold each other into the women we are destined to be.

Thank you to everyone who has supported me. Thank you for believing in my visions.

"There is a confidence behind being intelligent that surpasses any great fashion tip or great body… that nothing can replace."

-Jeannie Mai
Fashion Guru and Host

"At the end of the day, you are a beautiful person and you don't need to meet anyone else's standards. Just live for you!"
-Skai Jackson
Disney Actress

"I have used all of the manure that has been thrown on me as fertilizer to make me stronger."

-Eartha Kitt
Actress and Singer

"All women are goddesses, and it's just a matter of letting that goddess -power shine; and if you don't try to be the biggest and baddest damn goddess you can be, you are selling yourself short."

-Kimora Lee Simmons
Fashion Guru, Entrepreneur, Author

"I am learning every day to allow the space between where I am and where I want to be to inspire me and not terrify me."

- Tracee Ellis Ross
Actress

"There is something so special about a woman who dominates in a man's world. It takes a certain grace, strength, intelligence, fearlessness, and nerve to never take no for an answer."

-Rihanna
Singer

"If your dream only includes you, it's too small."

-Ave Duvernay
Television and Film Director

Contents

Introduction

For one reason or another, the day a girl hits eighteen she automatically feels like, "*I am a grown woman!*" Honey, please! It takes so much more to become a grown woman than two digits. My mother once told me that she wasn't a grown woman until she was forty! Forty?! That is a long way from eighteen. Although, I knew she wasn't serious, I understood what she meant. As women- scratch that - as humans, we go through so many different trials and tribulations. Those things build layers onto our character, and it builds us into the person we are destined to become. Yes, at eighteen, you are considered an adult; but, by far are you "grown". This takes time, experience, and a whole lot of blood, sweat, tears and fears; but if you focus on where you are going and who you want to become, it may make your life just a little bit easier.

"Oh... So Now You Think You're Grown" is specified for young women in their mid-teens, late teens and early twenties, but this book is relatable to most young women who's ready for a new shift in their lives. Each subject will relate to some part of your life. It is not to give you instructions on being a grown woman. Child, please, if that was the case, I would have been instructing myself. It's a *"Girl, been there, done that; take it from somebody who knows!"* kind of book. I'm not a guru, and I'm not a therapist. I am a girl from West Baltimore City who learned everything she knows through experience and being hard headed. Would I change my past? You know... I've asked myself that so many times. My first answer would be, *yes*; maybe a few things. But, if I changed my past to what I wanted it to be, I would not be writing this book for you right now. So, I guess my real answer would be *no*; although I can look back and dread some of those days. They have given me character and a voice to speak to the next girl and say, "Girl, don't do that."

As you have probably heard, life has a way of throwing you curve balls. You may even get hit with a bucket of lemons; and I'm sure you've heard what you should do with the lemons. Yes, you can make you some lemonade, and when you're done, sell them for one hundred dollars a cup and learn your worth. Now, that curve ball... the first one may catch you off guard. You may not see that one coming, but the second one...study it, watch the angle that it came from; meaning, learn from the experience so that when the next one comes (because there will be a next one), you will be a little more prepared for it. You may still strike out, but there will be a lesson in every curve ball that is thrown.

Throughout the book, you will notice that there are quotes in the middle of each chapter and a few homework assignments. The quotes are from women young and old that I admire one way or another. Or maybe I've read their quote and it stuck with me. Read the quotes and let them resonate in your mind. I know we all hate homework, but this is good homework. I promise! Each assignment will help you to gain a better understanding of who you are and who you want to be.

My goal is to prepare you for what will be a new adventure in your life...womanhood. And oh, what a ride it is! Just embrace it and enjoy the process. I wish I had listened to this advice the first time I said, "Ma, I'm grown!"

So, "Pretty Young Thang," let's get down to it!

But, first...

Before you begin to read this piece of gold in your hands, I suggest that you get to know yourself a little more. Some of these statements you may come back to at the end of the book, and that is totally fine. This will probably be one of the hardest things to do. One of the hardest questions I've ever had to answer was, "Who is Shanelle?" I honestly thought I had it down packed until I realized that my answers weren't real. I wasn't revealing my true self. I was revealing this girl who was all made up. I'm a tomboy in heels who loves a fly stiletto, but would die to own an all-black '76 Chevy with white interior and with the roof gone; but I will take a Mustang. Yes, that is who I am, but I also have pain. Pain that I hid from the outside world for years. There are so many things I want to do in this world. I have values and goals; and dreams bigger than this ratchet world can handle. I've been let down, which has caused me to have the spirit of rejection. It was hard to make friends because my confidence was low. I was a work of art on the outside, but, screaming for help on the inside.

I want you to get to know who you are from the inside out. Yes! At your age right now, the more you know and understand about yourself, the more aware you will be of your self worth and how you feel. Do not be a stranger to who you are. Love yourself enough to work on yourself. You are a masterpiece by design. Yes, you have flaws, and you always will, because you are human. We are all blank canvases that need splashes of color to build us and make us beautiful. That is what life is about.

Use the worksheet below to write basic information about yourself. This activity will be your foundation on this journey of "Who Am I?"

Who Am I?

My name is ______________________________.

I am_____years old.

My hobbies are ________________________________
____
____.

I am passionate about ___________________________.

My dream lifestyle is ____________________________
____.

The things I value in my life are ___________________
____.

If I could change three things about myself, they would be

1. ____
2. ____
3. ____

I would change these things because ______________
____
____
____
____.

My biggest fear is ______________________________
____
____.

I can overcome my fear by _______________________
____
____.

The person in my life who inspires me is______________,
because ____
____.

The things in life that inspire me are _____________
____
____.

If I could wake up every day and do only what makes me happy, I would ___________________________
____
____.

The things that make me sad are ________________

____

____.

I wish I could ____________________________

____

____.

Describe you. And, be honest (circle as many as you want).

Ambitious	Self Involved	Independent	Lazy
Inspiring	Motivational	Energetic	Spiritual
Passionate	Down to Earth	Fun Loving	Courageous
Greedy	Talented	Leader	Take-Charge
Optimistic	Boy Crazy	Loyal	Go Getter
Organized	Family Oriented	Thrill Seeker	Creative
Mediator	Messy	Innovative	Mouthy
Fire Cracker	Visionary	Selfish	Hard
Shy	Stubborn	Loner	Push Over
Tom Boy	Social Butterfly	Trustworthy	Boyfriend Stealer
Best friend Material	Materialistic (Are things the only thing important to you?)	I'm About My Paper $$	I'm Grown In these Streets

What is Your Personality Type

Check all that applies to you.

o **People Pleaser.**

I over extend myself to others. I want everyone to be happy. I have a hard time saying "no" when someone needs my help. I am the "fixer". There are times when I felt like others take me for granted.

o **I am a loyal friend.**

The people in my life know they can count on me.

o **I am Perfectionist.**

I can be very hard on myself. I am opinionated of others and myself at times.

o **I am a free spirited individual.**

Some people may say I am creative or the artsy type. I am always searching for my purpose or the meaning of life..

o **Self Aware.**

I am aware of my feelings and emotions. I listen to my inner self.

- **I am kind of an Introvert.**

  I don't mind being alone. I don't like people crowding my space. I am a private person.

- **Book Worm! That's me!**

  I love to read! Knowledge is everything. I spend time writing or reading. I am a thinker. I'm able to concentrate on things for a long period of time..

- **The Optimist.**

  I DREAM BIG. I have goals and I go after them. I have a big imagination. I visualize the things I want. Good vibes only!

- **I am the Leader of the Pack.**

  Just like Ariana Grande says, " I see it, I like, I want, I got it!" My friends call me for advice, because I think outside of the box. I am a take-charge kind of girl. I have a winning attitude and I stand out from everyone else. I aggressively go after my goals. Focused!.

- **" Can We All Just Get Along?"**

  You may call me a peacemaker. I try to stay clear of drama and in my own lane. There is no point in getting mad over spilled milk.

- **Yes, I'm a Little Shady.**

  If I like your boyfriend I just might take him. I will talk behind your back, better yet, I might say it to your face. Friend today; enemy tomorrow. Don't get on my bad side. I will make your life miserable. I hate when a girl thinks she's cute.

- **I Will Support You.**

  There is nothing like sisterhood! I support my friends. They can always count on me.

- **They Say I'm Bougie, I Say I have Standards.**

  I enjoy the finer things in life. There is nothing wrong with treating yourself well.

- **The Outsider.**

  I am the black sheep. It seems that wherever I go, (work, school, family) I am the outsider.

If I am missing something, you can list it below ____
____
____
____
____
____

You will learn more about yourself as you read this book. You will also become more aware of who you are becoming. Take time to evaluate yourself. Take inventory of who you are, what you want, and who you want to become. Be honest. This process is not to judge yourself. It is for you to have an understanding and make the necessary changes where needed.

Okay, let's get this thing poppin'!

"If I hadn't been told I was garbage, I wouldn't have learned how to show people I'm talented. And, if everyone had always laughed at my jokes, I wouldn't have figured out how to be so funny. If they hadn't told me I was ugly, I never would have searched for my beauty. And, if they hadn't tried to break me down, I wouldn't know that I am unbreakable."

-Gabourey Sidebe
Actress

LESSON ONE

Something Like the Beginning

Once again, JUST BECAUSE YOU'RE EIGHTEEN, IT DOES NOT MAKE YOU GROWN. I don't care if you move out of your parents' house. I don't care if you decided to get emancipated. You will learn what it means and how real it really is, but, before we get there, let's talk about...

The Concrete Jungle

Not New York City... high school! Yes, I refer to high school as the concrete jungle, but college and life after can be a jungle as well. So, take this advice for whatever chapter you are in at this moment and going forward in your life. Whether you're going to high school, starting college, or joining the rest of us in the working world, it can be exciting and stressful all at the same time. So, back to the high school experience - new people, new environment. The boys, look like grown men with mustaches and muscles. You may question if you are mentally ready or not. It's a different world.

There are a lot of decisions you have to make, and they will mold your future for the next four years and beyond that. So, try your best to make good decisions, and, of course, when you mess up…try, and try again.

My first year of high school was a complete mess. I tried to establish myself as a popular girl - fearless, no nonsense, blah blah blah blah blah. A distraction was what I became to myself. I spent more time trying to be someone that I wasn't just to leave an impression on people, not realizing that who I was would be good enough. I was very intelligent and creative, but I hid my gifts so that I could look like everyone else. I had a good relationship with most of my teachers and my principal, but I was still a hard-head, hot mess. I dealt with a lot at home, as well. After three years, my dad was back in my life after serving time in prison; and we were on completely different pages, which made my life a living… you know what I'm saying.

I got my work done for the most part, but my focus wasn't there. I focused more on my so called "friends" and what boy was the cutest, instead of my schooling. Now, this is not a lecture, but I'm just being real with you. Take care of your business and deal with all of the fluff later. It's good to have friends, but don't get so caught up in being popular and cool that it takes you away from what's important. It's nothing like a cute face with brains.

Focus

Again, don't forget about what you came to do. Yes, you are just a teenager, but there should be goals set in every stage of your life. Do not, I repeat DO NOT just blow with the wind. This will have you lazy and indecisive. Try new things, join a club, or get on a sports or academic team. Find something to do that will keep you focused and teach you discipline. Believe me when I tell you, you will need it. This is the time of your life where you can start thinking about what you want to be. When I say *thinking*, I mean just that. You will spend a lot of your time trying to figure out what you want to be when you "grow up". Your plans may change often between now and later, but there is no harm in getting a jump start. If you have an idea of what you may want to be, start doing a little research. Just Google it! Research the salaries and responsibilities of your career path. If you want to travel the world after high school or college, research the places you want to travel and how you can make it happen. It will give you a better understanding of who you are aspiring to become. You may decide that this is exactly what you want to do or you may just take a rain check and find something else. Either way, at least now, you have an idea. It's all in planning and taking action. I strongly believe in vision boards, to-do lists, and writing down your goals. These are exercises that will hold you accountable and keep you focused. We will get more into that later.

My Clique

So, there are a few pieces of advice that I wish I would have known, or, better yet, listened to during my teenage years. The first one would be: *Be careful with who you associate yourself with.* This is a lesson well learned, because I started off on the wrong foot! Again, I do not have regrets, because, like my father used to tell me, "Everything is a learning experience." And, man did I learn a lot! I attended the same high school as my oldest cousin, whom

I looked up to. She was a year older than me and a lot of her influence rubbed off on me. Don't get me wrong, I've always had my own mind. My parents did not raise a fool by a long shot, but if you are not careful, other people will rub off on you. This can be a good or bad thing. Do not cloud your own judgement or block your blessings by allowing someone else's bad habits to rub off on you.

Now, back to the older cousin. She already had a group of friends that she hung out with, so naturally, I hung out with them, too. They were not all bad, nor was my cousin, but I did step into some high school drama. And, because I wanted to make a name for myself and keep my friends, I put myself in a lot of situations that were not wise. I'm not blaming anyone else for any of my actions; I'm just saying that if I wasn't so busy trying to be known and liked I could have gotten a lot more done in my first year of high school. I definitely achieved my goal, because by the end of the school year I had gotten into a number of fights and disagreements that I could have avoided.

The second thing I learned, which really ties into the first lesson: *Do not play follow the leader!* Be your own person and have your own mind, because honey, the truth of the matter is, the person you're following may lead you right over a cliff! Better yet, they may have the hands that push you off the cliff! Seriously, he or she may not even be in your life in the next few years, months, days, or hours. So, use your own mind; and use it to the best of your ability. What you will find out later in life is that the people that you should be following were not the "clique" types. They do their own thing, go to class, socialize a little, but they never allow nonsense up in their space. Now that I look back, most of those people are successful today, in their own right.

Lesson three is: *Don't be the mean girl.* It's just not cool, and it AIN'T cute! Yes, I said "ain't!" Besides, you catch more bees with honey. Being a well-rounded, outgoing individual speaks volumes on so many levels. You can still be popular and be good to people. However, don't lose your fire either. There will always be someone in this world who will test how hot your fire is, so if need be, let them get burned in the most confident, yet, classiest way that you can. There is not always a need for screaming and fighting. People prey on the weak, especially when they are insecure; and if you look hard enough you will find that the "mean girl" is very insecure. She needs you to validate her importance. I have a post on my Instagram profile that says, "He who angers you controls you. The best revenge is living well." I will be the first to say that this statement is very true, however hard to swallow. I find myself still struggling with giving others my power. However, I can

Building relationships in high school can be a great experience. Those same relationships could be lifelong. Only time will tell which ones are genuine and long-lasting. Be yourself, and remember that it's always a give and take thing. If someone constantly needs something from you, but, is not a giver, then they are not a real friend or maybe they do not realize that all they do is take. Tell that person how you feel and if it doesn't change, then that means the relationship is one sided and should be checked at the door. Also, if you have to work so hard to be someone's friend - meaning not being yourself - or they have shady ways, then you need to leave them where they stand. Sorry, sweetheart, all I need is sunshine and palm trees; throw your shade "dat way" (straight face in my Quavo voice).

Working & School

I've always had a job; or should I say, found a way to get money. I started my first business at the age of ten. I did my girlfriends nails for twenty-five cents. At twelve, I started a babysitting business (my family actually trusted me with their kids). One of my eldest cousins is a registered nurse and she would pay me a hundred dollars for the whole weekend! I was "caked up" thanks to her. If you let my little brother tell it, he did the babysitting, but I honestly don't recall that. During the holidays, I offered my babysitting services for twenty dollars per kid while their parents went holiday shopping and celebrated the New Year. During my last summer of middle school, I worked at a newspaper warehouse for the Baltimore Sun Newspaper. My job was to roll newspapers and put them in the bag. By the time I was done, I hated the smell of newspaper. On top of that, they only paid about fifty cents a roll, so, I think I made about sixty dollars per day. I lied about my age for that job, up until I was actually sixteen. Wait a second. I am not, I repeat, I am NOT suggesting that you lie about your age for a job. I am only suggesting that sometimes a girl's gotta do what a girl's gotta do. All I knew was that I wanted to make money; and that meant by any means necessary. As long as I was not selling my "goodies" or my soul, it was pretty much a done deal for me. I worked all through high school. The grocery store, a clothing boutique, Wendy's, and because cosmetology was my focus at the time, I did hair and was a shampoo assistant.

Do I recommend working and going to school? It takes discipline, stamina, and focus to do so; and the bottom line is, knowledge comes first. There are different reasons to do so. Some kids get jobs because there is a sense of independence and there are those who work, because they lack in their household. There is nothing wrong with either, but there are pros and cons to working and going to school.

Pros

* You will bring home your own money.
* You may be able to give a little something to your parents to show appreciation.
* You will learn self-discipline, and how to budget and spend.
* You will build your resume early on.
* You will learn what jobs you like and don't like.
* You will be a dollar closer to purchasing your own car, if you don't have one.

* You will be able to save, save, save. You may want to take a trip after graduation or invest your money into something.
* You will learn to value your money and your time.
* You will not have to wait for someone to buy you what you want.
* You will learn professionalism early on.

Cons

* It can possibly distract you from school.
* Your social life will lack.
* It ties up most of your free time.

So, like I said, there are pros and cons, but working and going to school is really all about how you set your life up. And, you have the ability to do that! So, do not restrict yourself. Everything is goal setting and scheduling. You should also weigh your options and figure out what kind of job is for your personality and what will work for you. Will it be best to work a few days out of the week instead of a full week? Or should you wait until the summer? You will have to make a decision on what is more important to you.

Scheduling will consist of you writing down all of the things you have to do during the school year. If you are in after-school activities, studying, or if you have to watch your siblings on specific days, write down the days and times and whether or not they are flexible. When you go job-hunting you should schedule your days around that. For example; if you have cheerleading on Tuesdays and Thursdays, and games on Friday, then you know that Tuesdays, Thursdays and Fridays are out of the question. Which leaves you with Monday, Wednesday, Saturday, and Sunday. Church is Sunday morning, and school is Monday morning. You need to have time to prepare for school on Sunday evening; and you use Mondays to study. (Remember this is hypothetical. I don't know your life.) Saturday is pretty open, but you like to sleep late. So, this means that you have Wednesdays after 4pm, Saturday is open, and Sundays between 1pm and 9pm. Three days a week is enough time for a high school student to work, but to each his own.

Getting On Their Good Side

With your newly productive schedule: work, school, and being a teenager, please do not forget about the parents. I'm sure, that at this very moment, my father is rolling over in his grave, and my mother is probably rolling her eyes. I say this for a few reasons. I am a mother of two insanely beautiful girls who are still very young. Chloe'Rae is seven, and Harley is two. As new parents, my husband and I are still learning; and it is a process. My daughters have their own minds, and they are pretty outspoken. Chloe'Rae will tell us when she is unhappy, frustrated, scared, etc. No, seriously… she will literally call a family meeting in the bathroom to discuss her feelings. This happened a year ago, and I still haven't gotten over it; but moving on...As teenagers there are a few things that we lack when it comes to the parent-child relationship. Communication is one of them. It's okay to talk to your parents about what may be going on with you. You may not always like their response, but at least listen to see if you will get something out of it.

Building a trust and bond with your parents is vital. Now, don't get me wrong, some of you may not have an easy-going parent, but give it a trial run and see what you get out of an initial conversation. Talk to them about their past experiences; things you may be going through and see how they respond. If they are open to the conversation and you feel like they are being understanding, then keep it going! You will need these conversations and advice in the future, trust me! Another one of those things we lack is appreciation. There is nothing like a child showing some appreciation, even if it's every once in a while. When I say that, I mean, when you do get a job, treat your parents to something. Even if it's just Chic-fil-A or a movie. Tell them that you appreciate them. It matters; and it goes a long way! You will feel good about yourself, and it helps you to become a giver and not a person who always has her hand out.

Some of you may say, "I don't have that type of family," or "My parents don't want to listen to me," or "We don't get along." Okay… I understand that, because everyone has family issues here and there. Girl, I have been through the storm and back with both of my parents, but I promise you, things can change. First of all, TRY. If it doesn't work out, find someone that is close to you whom you trust and that will be a good mentor. But, continue to pray for a closer bond with your parents or guardians. Some days I didn't feel that I could talk to my parents at all. I honestly didn't trust them with my thoughts or feelings, but I had two aunts that I could talk to about anything. They helped me through a lot, but when I knew I could talk to my mom, I definitely did. My dad did more of the talking and lecturing, and even though I complained about it, every piece of information was a seed that he planted in me for my adult life. Although our relationship was love and war, he taught me most of the valuable lessons that I need today. I promise you, you will never know what you need until it's gone. Rest peacefully, Daddy!

Realistically speaking, some of us, including our parents, are prideful, arrogant and a little rebellious. None of these characteristics will help on either side of the relationship. It will only hurt it more. Your relationship with your parents will be the first relationship that you will ever have. It can possibly mold how you will treat your future relationships. In my opinion, family has to work on their relationships just as a couple or a marriage does. It's vital.

Last, but not least. Take time out of your busy, busy schedule to do some things around the house. And, do it without being asked! I promise you it will make your life so much easier. I was not the best at that, but when I did, I could see the difference in my parents' attitudes towards me.

The Pressure!

I promise you this will be short and sweet. There is a lot of pressure that comes with being a teenager in high school. You have peer pressure, pressure from your grades, boys, how you should look, speak, sound - the list goes on and on! Take a deep breath and a little time to relax. Do things that you enjoy and stay away from the negativity. Focus on what's important to you and do not get wrapped up in the foolishness.

I feel like young people don't get enough credit. We have all been in your shoes and we know how difficult it is to be a teenager or a young adult. Sometimes, as adults, we forget. But, girl! Just know that I get it! I really, really do! I know that you may be having an identity crisis. I've had at least fifty! I know that your parents don't understand you and that some days you feel alone. I hope and pray that you do not let the pressure of this world or the pressure that you have on yourself overwhelm you. Pull yourself together and keep it moving. It is going to all work out, if you let it!

I remember watching an interview of Michelle Obama. I believe she was at a college speaking to the young women. One thing that she said that stuck with me was if she had focused on boys, she would have been distracted from her goals, and the President would not be her husband. She is basically saying: don't get distracted by a cute face. I, for one, allowed that distraction in my life. Now, I am still with my high school sweetheart; however, if I decided to do that part of my life differently, I would not have given him, or any other guy I dated, so much of my time. I was infatuated with my high school sweetheart; and puppy love was in the air! Nothing else mattered as much as being around him. I would definitely tell the young me to focus, spend more time with friends, and holla at him on the weekends. But, you live and you learn. Just know that every move you make will have some kind of effect on your future. If you are not applying yourself and putting in the work to get into your dream school, start your business or move to that city; you are delaying your dreams from coming true. So, find balance; and don't allow the pressure around you to distract you from your plan.

Your Homework:

What are some things that you can change after reading this chapter? Why? What would you do differently?

Do you have goals for this school year or the next four years? If so, what are they?

How can you improve your daily schedule to have more time in your day?

____

____

____

How is your energy level daily? High or low? Why?

____

____

____

What are you lacking from your day to day activities that can help you improve?

____

____

____

____

Where do you feel the most pressure in your life comes from? What can you do to keep it under control?

In my opinion, everyone should have a planner if they have a demanding life. Yes, that includes high school and college students; because your life is demanding. However, if you do not have a planner, here is a way to schedule your daily to-do list. You can either make it once a week, or daily. It's best to make it the night before your week or day starts. I have learned that when I do not have my to-do list together, my day is all over the place and I am more busy than productive. Meaning, I am moving without intention. By the end of the day, I realize I haven't gotten anything done.

My daughter Chloe'Rae is my saving grace. Both of my girls were literally put here for me. Like God picked them out and said, "Yeah these two will set Shanelle straight!" Chloe'Rae is my in-home life-coach! In case you don't know; a life coach is someone who helps you to get your life together. They help you to strategize on your goals and make them happen. She sets me straight. First, let me remind you that she is seven. One day we were driving in the car and I was reciting to myself all of the things I needed to get done. She looks over and says to me in a soft, yet, stern voice, "Ma, don't you want to be successful?" I replied, "Yes, I want to set you and your sister up to do whatever your hearts desire." She said, "Well, Mommy, you have to focus. You try to do too much at one time. In one day, you call clients, work on your book, work on a stage play, look for a house, and write a script. You can't do everything at one time. Choose one and get it completed; that is how you are going to be rich!" I had to stop the car. I couldn't believe that my seven year old was kicking knowledge to me. Girl, she got me all the way together! Every word she said was very true. You cannot get anything done if you are working on a thousand things at one time. Choose one and get it done. I must admit this has been very hard for me. Because I am a creative and a visionary, my mind runs consistently with new ideas. You will surely achieve everything you need to if you focus and set deadlines.

Here is an example:

To-Do List (Saturday)

* Wash clothes
* Study for test
* Clean room
* Get to work - scheduled from 4pm to 9pm
* Meet Mia at the movies at 9:30pm

This is just an idea. You can put the highest priorities first, and the lowest last. You can put a star next to the most important, or you can just put a time deadline next to each. If I start early, I will try to finish all of my errands by 12pm. That will free up the rest of my day to write a little more, spend time with my husband, or just relax until the kids get home. Do what works for you. Yes, you should have time to just chill. That's really the whole point. If you put yourself on a schedule, you will free up so much of your time to do whatever you want. My last piece of advice on this subject is to not over do it. Do not make yourself so "busy" that you burn yourself out. I know, because I've done it. Be productive with your time and pace yourself.

Chapter Journal

This is a moment for you to have an emotional dump! Write whatever you are thinking or feeling. This is your moment. Go!

"It's up to you to be responsible for how you feel if you're not happy. Your happiness lies in your hands. You can't rely on a man to make you happy or complete you. That starts with you."

-Taraji P. Henson

When life puts you in a tough place, don't say "Why me?" Say, "Try me."

Miley Cyrus

"There are no ceilings when the sky is the limit."

-Hillary Clinton

"I like to be scared. I don't like feeling like,
"Oh, this is going to be a walk in the park."
If I ever get to that place. I'll just stop acting.

Taraji P. Henson

LESSON TWO

"The Real World" Slaps You in the Face

So, let's fast forward. High school is over and now we get to the meat of the sandwich…adulthood! All of that, "I can't wait to be 18..." may be the last thing on your mind, or you may be ready to dive right in. Either way, I hope you have prepared yourself mentally, physically, and spiritually, because it's about to get real!

First thing's first…just know that everyone's experience is different, but my goal is to prepare you the best way I can, just in case you are hit with a similar situation. After being out of high school for a few years I decided to go back to my old high school in Baltimore, Carver Vocational - Technical High School. I have a very close relationship with my cosmetology teacher and she allowed me to come into class and talk to the girls about life post-graduation. We did vision boards, talked about goals and aspirations, and much more. My mission was to inform and inspire them. Hopefully, they carried some of the things we talked about. Now, it's your turn.

What Happens After High School

Walking across that stage felt so good. I could not believe that my years in grade school were finally over. I would finally get out in this world and show the people what I was made of. I'm calling the shots! I'm a grown woman!

Not.

The first day after graduation, I was still on cloud nine; but two weeks later, I was just confused. I knew I was going to college, but I wasn't sure of what I wanted to do. I spent many, many days staring at my bedroom wall saying, *"What am I going to do now?"* Then the next question was, *"How will I spend my summer?"* My mother would wake me up early every morning, and I knew that was her way of saying, *"You better find a job, a hobby, or something."* A summer with no money and no goals is not a fun summer. Especially for a girl like me.

This is a time in your life when you have a lot of decisions to make. Now, if you played your cards right during high school, you may have saved up some money to travel with friends, buy a car, or you may already have a job for the summer. Or maybe you have already decided on what college you will be attending and what your major will be. In that case, you're good. Just stack your paper, baby sis. On the other hand, if you don't have a plan, no money, and no job, I'm going to need you to get on your feet! That's right, rise and grind baby, because before you know it, the summer will be over and you will still be confused and broke. Enjoy and celebrate your independence; however, your celebration should not last the whole summer. Grab and secure your bag!

College? Job? Career? Passion?

I want you to see me as a big sister; and as a big sister, I'm going to tell you the truth. College is not for everybody. Yes, I've gone to college, and a lot of my friends graduated with bachelors and associates. It's a wonderful thing; but, I cannot say that it's always relevant. Now, if you plan to be a doctor or lawyer, those kinds of careers will require you to go to college. For example; my little sister is a pastry chef. She is the youngest in one of the most prestigious hospitals in Baltimore City. She is nineteen years old and has been working there since she graduated high school. She has been baking cakes since she was about three or four, and I'm not exaggerating. She now has her own business selling desserts, while still employed at the hospital. One day, she called me and said she was going to go to college for culinary arts. I was so confused! I can understand taking business courses to further her business, but she has already achieved so much and she has learned a ton through experience. So why not go to Italy or somewhere else to intern or gain more experience? And believe me, traveling is not an issue (she went to China at the age of sixteen for ten days… at sixteen I would have cried every day to go home). I still have debt from college; along with so many others who went to college and are not working in the field that they majored in. There are doctors and lawyers who struggle with paying back student loans. Please, do not get me wrong. I am not anti-college at all. It's a great experience, and you will learn different cultures and meet lifelong friends. If you want the experience…great; if you are going after a career that definitely requires college, or if school will help guide your path, then, by all means, go for it. I'm just saying, if you are going to go, just do your research and make sure you *need* to go. Time and money are both valuable, so make wise decisions.

Jobs... ugh, I am not a 9 to 5 kind of girl! I can't stand it; but, once again, if you are going to do something, have a plan and an exit strategy. Do not get comfortable or complacent. Always have a plan. If you are in college, this job will hold you over until you graduate and get into your desired field; unless you are already there and love it. Or you may be saving up to purchase a house or houses. Whatever you are doing with that job, just remember that it is a tool. It should be used as just that. I can honestly say, that there have been times when I didn't use my J-O-B correctly. When you begin your job search, have your plans in mind. Meaning, if you plan to be a veterinarian, you should get a job at the zoo, a pet store, or an animal hospital. If the jobs that are related to your plan are unavailable, then get a job to just make money until what you want comes through. You can also volunteer on the side just to get the experience in your field. Try to stay away from doing things just for the money, because it will become a habit and dissatisfying. As time goes on, you will notice that your resume is filled with random jobs with no focus; which I've learned does not look good when you finally get to the "job" you want. So, save yourself the headache.

Here is the problem I faced: I'm an artist and an entrepreneur. If I can't produce and create beautiful things, I get crazy. For me, a regular nine to five in an office building is like going to the cemetery to lay flowers. I would get fed up and quit a job without considering my goals, my plan, or the fact that my bills were due; and believe me, I would feel it later. If you don't plan to be in a place forever, plan your exit from the beginning and work your way to it. Your parents may not agree with me, and my advice is not written in stone. These are strictly my opinions. I just know that there is nothing more satisfying than doing something that you absolutely love while you make money. That's the ultimate success!

So, When Are You Moving Out?

At the age of nineteen, I moved out on my own. My family was driving me crazy and I wanted my own space. At this time, I took a year off of school and I was working full time at a collection agency. For a girl my age, the money was pretty good. I was once again on cloud nine. I had a two-bedroom townhouse, a brand new car, and a Shitzu puppy named, Neiko, whom I absolutely adored. I was independent and doing it all on my own; and it felt good! I could come and go as I pleased, there were no rules, and my house was decorated with a red suede sofa, multi colored chandeliers, wall to wall carpet, a king size bed and large pictures of Aubrey Hepburn and Marilyn Monroe. My house was lit; to say the least! At nineteen, I felt like I had it made. Everything was going great, but there were two things that went wrong. The first one was, I didn't quite think it all through. I had enough savings in the bank for at least two months, but I received a call from the leasing office that I had to pay more rent for moving in during the middle of the month. Which means I had to use what I had saved. Secondly, one day I woke up and realized that this is forever! I'm laughing about it now, but in a way, it scared me, because I stepped out so quickly to be an adult that even though I had my own place and was free, I didn't have time to make any mistakes, because I had bills. So, I wasn't actually free. I became a slave to my bills! My friends were going to Miami for spring break, and I was working to pay my bills while they were working for clothes, savings, and trips. So, the lesson here is…if you are going to move out early, make sure you stack your money to the ceiling, have enough for emergencies, but also put some away for playtime so that when you do move on your own, you don't feel like you are living paycheck to paycheck. You have money saved, money to play, and money to spend. This all starts with a budget (we will get into that later). But, the real advice is… STAY HOME! STACK MONEY! HAVE FUN! STACK MONEY! LEARN HOW THE WORLD WORKS! STACK MONEY! BUILD YOUR CREDIT! STACK MONEY! PAY SMALL BILLS! STACK MONEY! TRAVEL THE WORLD! STACK MONEY! I'm telling you some good stuff, baby girl. JUST STACK MONEY! While you're stacking, keep what you have in your pocket a secret. Your dollar signs are no one's business except yours. As long as you can cover your side of the bills, that's all they need to know. The more they know, the more they want.

A Letter to Young Mothers

I do not know if any of you are young mothers. I am speaking on this topic because I know a few, and I also know that the world can count you out. I am not, what-so-ever, glorifying "young mothers;" however, this book is for all young girls and young adult women. Just know that your walk will be a little different, but that does not mean that you should stop; and do not make your baby an excuse. You still have the ability to do all things. I know young mothers that have become very successful in their own right, and they didn't sell their souls to do it. They just bossed up and got it done. I also know young mothers who used their baby as an excuse to be lazy and throw pity parties. They have nothing, and continue to be lazy and throw pity parties. So, don't be that girl, everything in this book applies to you, too. Make goals for you and your child. Even if they take time, knock them out one by one. I was not a young mother, but I am a mother, and the only difference is the age we started. The struggle is still real. If you are ashamed, get over it and move on, because your baby does not want to embarrass you; it is just here to love you. So, make your way and set your mark in this world. It all starts now!

Time Flies So Get on the Grind Now

Whether you've moved out or decided to stay home, you should have a plan set in place for your life. I know,

I know- I used the word "plan" a thousand times. It's cool; but, I bet you my last dollar it will be the one thing you take from this book. Yes, plans change, but you should have an idea of what you are going to do for at least the next two to three years. I promise that if you don't, your life will be all over the place. I had a plan that I was so-so going through with. In high school, I studied cosmetology. My plan was to get my license after high school and go to college for business so that I could open up my own salon and eventually become a celebrity stylist. I got my license and I went to college for business. God obviously had other plans for my life, because now, I am on a different path. One day I had an epiphany that I should be working in front of the camera and not as the lead hair stylist. So, I slightly switched gears and started studying acting, which had been my childhood dream. All of this to say…make a decision and go for it. It may not be the end all be all, but it may be your stepping stone to something else. If you have to use your other gifts to get to your purpose and passion, that is totally fine; but don't forget about your plans. A plan will help you to move with purpose and elevate you.

Start recording your goals. Write them down. What is your six-month plan, one-year plan, five-year plan? Look at them every day, if you can, and move on them. They may not always fall the way you expect, and there will be days that you are discouraged and feel defeated, but all of this will make you stronger and build your character. Do not be afraid to fail or make mistakes, because when the fire goes out, you will rise out of the ashes as a different person.

I'm going to be honest. I spent most of my teenage years and twenties being a very indecisive person. Because of that, I missed out on a lot of opportunities. Do not take your youth or your time for granted. The next time you look up to make a decision you will be twenty, then twenty-five, and then thirty. Try your best to make each step strategic. Do not waste time with thinking, "I'm still young. I still have time." Most people who say that or believe that do not achieve much in their lives. You have some that achieve things late in their lives, but more than likely, they started working on it at an earlier age, or they put so much focus into it that they made it to their destination in a "timely manner". Let me be clear…it's not about getting to your destination quicker it's about progressing towards it. You can have your dream car and dream house, or travel the world at the age of thirty, maybe even 25, if you start putting your plans in motion now. You will make mistakes; and you will realize that some things are not for you, but it's better to experiment and take chances now. Weave out what will and will not work. Don't wake up at forty and realize that you missed out on so much because you were too lazy or too scared. Just do it! Time is of the essence, and these days, it moves faster than the speed of light. Get on the grind NOW!

Bills! Bills! Bills!

The price to pay for being a grown, independent woman is bills and hard work. It sounds great to pay your bills and do your own thing. Then you realize this is forever. That means that you have to take on a discipline called responsibility. You have to make adult choices and sacrifices that will not only help you to survive, but to thrive! To thrive is the key! Survival is just living day by day trying to make it. Believe me, it does not feel good! What does feel good is having control over your lifestyle. There is no other feeling like it. My twenties were an emotional roller coaster. Some days I was up, and some days down. At one point, I had a plan, and then it all fell to pieces, but I had to figure out how to put myself back together to become a successful woman in my own right. Later, I realized that I was the cause for the majority of my plans falling through. While I am writing this book, I am going through a few storms, but because I have had so many challenges, it has prepared me to make better decisions than before. I can't let storms stop me from getting to my purpose; no matter how big. So, you want to feel free like a bird, not stress about money, take a few trips; it is possible if you plan well. That starts with putting together a budget.

Most people shy away from budgets. They believe they have control over their money or they can keep all of their plans in their heads. My senior year in high school, my cosmetology teacher, Ms. Robinson, ceased our regular cosmetology assignments. She felt that we needed to learn about real life; and I totally agreed! One thing I deeply believe is that our school systems do not prepare us for real life! How to budget, networking, being an entrepreneur... I just don't understand how U.S. History is going to teach me how to make money or build a solid team around me. If you want to be the president or governor it makes sense, but what about the rest of us? This is just my opinion, so don't go back to school and tell your U.S. History teacher that, "Shanelle said I shouldn't be here." That is one phone call I do not need, okay!? Anyway, back to Ms. Robinson. She assigned two budget projects; the first one was a budget with a baby. Of course, that one got a lot of backlash, because we had pregnant teens in class. However, I'm sure that this project has helped them in their future. The second project was also a budget plan. It included everything from monthly rent down to monthly entertainment. She had us to budget down every single thing in our lives. We had to have a total gross of monthly income; and the way we came up with that was by researching the job we were interested in having and where we wanted to live. That project changed my life! That was the first time someone had actually influenced my future in that way. She made me want to be a responsible adult. She made me want to get up and do something and to be cautious about my spending.

If you want to live a good life and not feel like you are a prisoner to your bills, please budget your money. Do the best you can. If you start practicing now, it will become second nature as you mature. You may not make a lot of money, but if you can budget two-hundred dollars and spend it wisely, you will have the ability to do even better with two-thousand or two-million.

As women, we like to spend money - it's a given. Hair, nails, makeup, clothes, shoes - these are must-haves. Looking good and feeling good is aligned together. But, this is where the problem comes in… we overdo it and over spend. You do not have to have three pairs of shoes a month; and sometimes you may have to settle for a manicure instead of a full set. Sometimes, that's just how it is; so, get that twenty-dollar mani and pedi deal and keep it moving. However, when you get your coins up, treat yourself to a shopping spree and spa day. You can look good without breaking the bank every month. There should be more money in your bank account than what you are actually spending.

With budgeting comes saving. I do believe in saving. You never know what great opportunity may come about that will inspire you to invest. For example, your friends may decide they want to go on a big trip somewhere; I don't know let's say, Mexico. Instead of penny pinching to go, you may have already saved money to pay at least half on that trip. That brings me to my next point. Don't spend all that you save. Spend some, save some. I have what I call an "opportunity savings." I was inspired by Ms. Patrice Maven. She is an expert on saving, spending, and investing money. Instead of having an emergency fund, she has an Opportunity Fund. Emergency fund sounds so draining and uninspiring, but an opportunity savings will motivate you to want to save for something big! I also do cash envelopes, and my good ol' piggy bank (she's gold…I love it!). I have savings accounts for different reasons: opportunity, family, vacation, my girls, investing, maintenance, and my business. That way, I am very specific as to what I am saving for. These particular accounts are online accounts. Online accounts are easy to put money in, but harder to get them out. This is great and it will help you, because the hassle of taking out money would mean waiting a few days; so just keep your cute little fingers off of it - the shoes can wait! The cash envelope is also a good tool. Now caution; if you live with other people, you should hide it in a safe place, unless you know they won't bother with it. Use your cash envelopes the same way. Write on each envelope what the money will be used for and deposit the money in the envelopes. If you need easy access for a bill or you want to buy something for yourself, this would be a perfect technique for you, but you need to discipline yourself; and girl, it AIN'T easy.

We talked a little bit about investing your money. Of course, with budgeting and saving also comes investing. When I was in high school, I was very good at saving my money. The problem was, I made some dumb choices with the money I saved. I remember I saved three hundred dollars from my checks working at the grocery store. I used that money to buy a prepaid phone! The whole thing! I felt like I was the only girl in high school without a phone, so I brought my own. Two problems: it wasn't worth it, and it was prepaid! That one word makes me cringe! I know you're pretty young, so I will define prepaid. In order to use the phone, you will need to buy a money card, like a Green Dot card, to load minutes on your phone; but you had free nights and weekends. Every minute you spent on the phone during the day was a loss. It was ridiculous. I spent so much money per week on buying minutes. A smart kid at fifteen would have used that money to pay for driving school, or even a new wardrobe. I brought a phone that I could barely use. What made it worse was that my father brought me the very same phone, with a plan! (Only so he could take it back when he felt like it; but that's beside the point.) I still saved up and put myself through driving school a few months later. The point is, make good decisions with your money; or at least try to. These days, young adults are investing in stocks. That is what's up! We spend money with these companies every day; why shouldn't we own a piece of it? Think about it. Your favorite pair of sneakers, your favorite store, restaurant, brand or whatever. You can invest in your own happiness; and, as I stated earlier, an experience is always a good investment. I read about a young boy a few years ago named Damon Williams, who only wore Nike sneakers. He was fifteen back then. He invested in Nike, and at that time, he owned fifty shares of Nike with a worth of fifty- thousand dollars. At fifteen! That was over seven years ago. I'm sure you get the picture.

One more thing... credit cards! Honey, listen…my first year out of high school, I became the credit card queen! I didn't have the knowledge that I have now, but I wish I did. I wish I had listened to my mother when she said credit cards are the devil. Now, to be honest I don't agree with that. It's how you use them. When you turn eighteen, you will receive applications from a number of credit card companies, and you will be offered one every time you shop in your favorite stores. Here is the pick-up line: "Would you like to open a new credit card with us today? You will save fifteen percent off your purchase." Then your face glows up and you fall into the consumer trap. Don't worry girl, it has happened to the best of us! I, for one, had a credit card for each of my favorite stores… Victoria Secret, Nordstrom, even Ashley Stewart. In case you don't know; Ashley Stewarts is a store for plus size women. I had no business having a credit card there! They had the cutest jewelry, and I have a few beautiful, voluptuous women in my family to shop for. On top of that, I had bank credit cards. My wallet was full, and so were my balances on each of them! I paid for my first college spring break experience on a credit card!

If you are going to get a credit card, make sure you understand what that means. It means, IT'S A LOAN. You have to pay it back and you have to pay interest or it will destroy your credit score, which you will cherish when you are ready to make big moves in your life. You don't need a credit card for every store you shop in. I know it may make you feel all grown up when you open your wallet, but one bank credit card is more than enough. Think about credit cards like this; that three dollars that you used on your credit card to buy a cheeseburger was a loan. You took out a loan for three dollars! Does that make sense? No it doesn't. Just use cash, if you don't have it, then fine; use the credit card, but make sure you have money coming in to pay the three dollars off. Believe me, I know.

Bottom line, use one credit card, and as soon as you get paid, either pay it off, or at least, pay half. You have a minimum; but pay more if you can. Also, never close out your credit cards; it looks bad on your credit. Just cut it up and forget about it. I got all up in my feelings after I paid off all of my credit cards. I cut them up, and then called each one and closed them out; but again, I didn't know any better.

Please understand, I am not a financial guru or advisor by a long shot! I am just a girl who has made enough mistakes for the both of us. Not just in this aspect, but in other parts of life, as well. I just want to share the experience so that you will make better choices. Like I said, I'm like your big sister in a book.

I will leave you with this… Read books about money. If you are not an avid reader, like myself, then search Youtube or Google. Gain some financial intelligence. You will thank me later.

Here is an example of a budget plan. This is one of the best tools I've been given. Although, I have not always used it to the best of my ability, it has given me a foundation to how to manage my money.

I found this worksheet on Google. The items on this budget sheet may not be what you are budgeting for. For example, you may have student loans if you decide on college or you may want to take a little of your check to treat yourself to a pair of shoes with your high school paycheck. Pinterest is also a great reference to get free printable budgets. You can get a blank one and fill in your items or you can scratch out and substitute. In high school you will not need all of these things, but as you move into adulthood you will need to budget for the majority of them.

MY MONTHLY BUDGET

MONTHLY EXPENSE	AMOUNT	DUE DATE
HOME		
Mortgage/Rent		
Repairs		
UTILITIES		
Electric		
Gas		
Water, Sewer & Garbage		
Phone (Cell)		
Phone/Cable/Satellite		
Internet		
Other		
TRANSPORTATION		
Car Payment		
Gas		
Repairs/Maintenance		
INSURANCE		
Car Insurance		
Health Insurance		
Other		
DEBT PAYMENTS		
Credit Card		
Other		
MISC.		
Groceries		
Personal Care (clothing, shampoo, etc.)		
Household Items (cleaning supplies, toilet paper)		
TOTAL DUE		
TOTAL WAGES		
TOTAL LEFTOVER		

Homework

What part of this chapter really resonates with you?

What are some things you can change after reading this chapter?

What are your plans after high school? If you are not sure, write down a few things that interest you. For example: Traveling, moving to a new city, going to college, pursuing your passion or career goals; whatever comes to mind.

Is there a career path that interests you? If so, have you done any research, such as, salary or the necessary steps to get there? If you have, what are they? If not, use this space to do your research.

Where do you see yourself at the age of twenty-one, twenty-five or even thirty? Pick one age or all.

____

____

____

Will this bring you happiness? ____________________

Will it pour greatness into you? ___________________

Is this setting you up for a great future? ____________

Being fearless isn't being 100% not fearful. It's being terrified, but you jump anyway.

-Taylor Swift
Singer/Songwriter

LESSON THREE

Make Your Mark

So, my daughters have a Disney movie called the "*Good Dinosaur*." We watched it during movie night one night, and in the beginning of the movie, the youngest and smallest dinosaur was too small and immature to do the things that his siblings did. His father had built a large tomb to store their food, and on it, each of them would leave a paw print, which symbolized them leaving their mark for doing something great. The small dinosaur had not left his mark, yet. Not only because he had not done anything yet, but he also did not feel worthy to do so. We will get into worthiness later, but, right now, let's focus on leaving your mark in the world.

We were put on this planet with purpose. Your job on this planet is to fulfill that purpose. Period, point blank. Your life will never be lived to its full potential until you walk into your purpose. No, it's not going to come slap you in your face and say, "Hey, I'm your purpose!" It may show up in your passion or your job. Most of the time, it will show up in your gift.

For example, I've always known that I was different. I knew that I was not put here to be a doctor or nurse or any kind of white-collar job. I have always been an entrepreneur, creative, a problem solver, and I've been writing short stories and poems since a young age. I discovered my love for acting at the age of five after watching Raven Symone on *The Cosby Show*, and meeting Jada Pinkett at my cousin's house in Baltimore. I chose to be a hairstylist in high school, because I thought it would be the easiest and most interesting trade, but, there was no passion at all in the beginning. I grew my passion for helping people and young women discover their best selves after having my own experiences. I am the eldest of about twenty cousins and three siblings. As I said before, I lecture to them all of the time for obvious reasons.

How does all of these things work together? Well, they don't actually all work together, but they all have something in common. All of these gifts have allowed me to minister to others in my own way. I have inspired others to push forward with their dreams while styling their hair. I've shown people who they are and who they could be while in character in a stage production or writing books and creating my own path. I've taught young girls how to present themselves and love themselves while mentoring; and being the eldest of so many has given me the opportunity to practice this gift on them. I was put here to motivate, inspire, and help others through my creative gifts. This is the mark that I believe I will be leaving on this world. It may take time for you to figure out your purpose, but if you continue to strive through life your purpose will be aligned with your passion and gifts in some shape or form.

You've Been Blessed...Now, Be A Blessing

I consider myself a spiritual person. I believe that God gives us a life to put back into. I also believe that when you have been blessed in whatever way, you should bless someone else. It doesn't have to be financially, it can be a word of encouragement or time. I consider this book a blessing, because I'm giving you my experiences as tools to learn from and to use to your advantage. The world is formulated around giving and receiving not just receiving. Even if you are waiting for something to happen in your life or you don't feel like yourself today, you should still be able to encourage someone else or help someone if you can. It will make you feel better about yourself.

Just Let Me Be Great

I will say believe in yourself and have confidence a lot in this book, because it is very important. You have a gift; we all do. In order to make your mark in this world, you have to discover your gift and your purpose. This may take some time, but they say that whatever you do with the least amount of effort is your gift. However, your gift may not always be your passion; if it is, that is great. The bottom line is, whatever you were sent here to do, do it! Have enough confidence in yourself and don't shy away from whatever it may be. One of my favorite Beyonce' songs is, "I Was Here." That song is geared specifically toward her making her mark in this world. She found her purpose and she tackled it with aggression. The goal is not to be popular, have twenty million followers and a thousand likes; it's to leave a legacy that says, "I was here."

You're Going to Be Successful Whether You Want to Be or Not, Shanelle Williams!

This subtitle was my mother's favorite line when she was disappointed in me. It has stuck with me over the years, especially when I feel like I am failing. Success does not mean being a millionaire. Truthfully, everyone has their own definition of what success is. Success to me, is being free enough to do what I love while being compensated my worth, and experiencing all the beauties of life, being healthy, and being filled with joy. So, it's not always a money thing. For me, it's a mind, body, soul, and my coins thing. A lot of people with money are not happy. For example; Robin Williams was a phenomenal character actor (if you don't know who he is, he played *Mrs. Doubtfire*; and if you never saw this classic, I'm going to need you to see it, along with *Jumanji* and every other Robin Williams movie). I'm sure he was pretty wealthy after the hundreds of movies he was a part of, but he suffered with depression, along with so many other rich and famous people. Success goes so much deeper than money.

Believe Beyond Believing!

Believing in yourself can be so hard to do sometimes. There have been times when I was an inch away from giving up on my dreams of being an actress, producing films, writing this book, and others. It's a struggle, and it does not come easy; and if it comes too easy, it may not last. The thing about trials and tribulations is, they were put here to build your character and make you stronger. The moment that you give up, you lose your power. What I have learned is that you get back what you put out and you can't allow your negative thoughts to get in the way of achieving your goals.

I have been working on the same project for seven years now. In 2010, I linked up with a guy I met on a music video set and we collaborated on a script I was writing. He was a film student; he was the director and cinematographer, and I was the producer, lead actor, and screenwriter. After casting the roles and booking locations, we started filming. A month into production, he was no longer able to get equipment. I thought my life was over! I had to call all of these actors and tell them we were no longer filming. I tried to use the footage for promotion and could not get it from the guy. Finally, I gave up and put it to the side. Later that year I found out I was pregnant with Chloe'Rae. I was nervous, I was scared, and I felt like my life was going to be on hold. Rewinding back before my pregnancy, I was aggressively pursuing acting. I lived in New York and traveled to LA for auditions. I was constantly on the move, so you can understand why my pregnancy surprise was scary.

During my pregnancy, I tried to figure out what I could do to keep myself connected creatively. So, I took my script and I converted it into a book. It was a long process. There were so many setbacks during this process. My computer crashed, my screen was cracked, writers block, I had to relocate, the baby crying for hours; any and everything to slow me down. It took me three years to finish that book, but I envisioned the end result and I would not stop until I got there. I finished it, and I am now back to producing the series for it. I have, once again, come into a few detours in the road, but I will not stop until it is on a television screen. That is my word! I feel this way about everything that I do. It may take a little time and there may be signs telling you to quit, but if you believe in something with your whole heart and soul, it will not let you quit. Tyler Perry says, "Believe beyond believing," and I truly believe in that. It's so easy to give up on something, but, push through and believe you were put here to make you mark.

Becoming someone in this world should be one of the most important things on your life's agenda. It may sound like it's not a big deal now and living day by day is not too bad, but when you are twenty-five, and then, thirty, you will wish you would have spent a little more time trying to become somebody. You don't have to wait until you're twenty-one to make an impact in this world… you can start now!

Homework

What are some things you can change after reading this chapter?____

Everyone has their own idea of what success means to them. For me, success means to have peace, to wake up every day and do what I love, to make beautiful memories with my family and friends, and get paid handsomely. Now...there are a lot of people who believe that money, and money alone, is success. There are a lot of wealthy people that have no peace, no friends or family. That's not success; that's just a miserable person who figured out how to make money. What does success mean to you?

____

____

____

____

What mark do you want to leave on this world? How will you begin to set your mark?

____

____

____

____

When you were a little girl, what did you want to be when you grew up?

____

____

Do you still want this? Why or why not?

____

____

____

"I embrace mistakes; they make you who you are."
-Beyonce'

"There is no limit to whatever a woman can accomplish."
-Michelle Obama
(My FLOTUS forever!)

"Life is too short. You need to make sure you are happy with whatever you are doing.
-Loni Love
Actress, Comedian, and Host of "The Real"

"The best thing about life is the chance to keep on doing it."
-Lena Horne
Singer and Actress

LESSON FOUR

Do Not Exist...Live!

I will be one to say I have spent some time in my twenties just existing, but if you ask the people around me, they would probably say that is very far from the truth. I have always been the "take care of business" type. I did not spend a lot of time simply enjoying myself like I could have. This is where my lack of life balance came in; and one thing you will need is balance. Don't work so hard that you forget to play! I spent a great portion of my twenties working or focusing on my relationship that I forgot to go on girlfriend trips and enjoy the things in life that I loved to do so much. While my girlfriends were going to Miami for vacation, I was at work on my 9 to 5 paying my never-ending bills. When I finally had the chance to go to Miami, it was alone and for a film festival. Now, don't get me wrong, that was a wonderful experience which I plan to have more of. The point that I am trying to make is, business trips should balance out with a simple "good time" vacation. If not a vacation, just take time to catch up with friends and hangout. Just don't forget to enjoy life. I have been guilty for taking life way too seriously. So, girl, stop and smell the roses.

Have an "Eat, Pray, Love" Moment

You're probably too young to have any interest in the movie, "*Eat, Pray, Love.*" Julia Roberts portrayed a woman who felt stuck in her marriage and in her everyday life. She wanted excitement and adventure. After having a talk with God, she decided to get a divorce and spend one year traveling the world. She went to Italy, India, and Bali. Her experience changed who she was in the beginning to a woman of peace, joy, and confidence. This movie was life changing for some of us. My point is this. Take a chance to step back and experience life to the best of your ability; because before you know it, that moment will pass. Girl, believe me when I tell you time waits for nothing or no one so you better get it while you can! Get out here and experience new places, eat different foods, learn a new culture…travel! Don't miss out on opportunities that will give you a memory of a lifetime.

You may be too young to do it all, but when you get the opportunity, don't pass it up.

In my early twenties, I worked at an upscale salon in Baltimore. There was a girl there whom I admired. She was, and still is, a great hairstylist. She didn't care for me too much, but she said something to me one day that inspired me. I was a brand-new hairstylist, so I did not have clientele; I sat in the salon day after day waiting for walk-ins and giving out cards every once in a while. One day she told a story of how her sister traveled to California to work and she turned to me and said, "That's what you need to do. You need to do something!" At that moment, I could have gotten upset with her, but instead I heard her loud and clear. At that moment in my life, I was unclear of what my future plans were. I had lost my dad, I had a house with bills, and was new to the beauty industry, so salon money was not happening. I needed inspiration. I needed to see something different than Baltimore's Inner Harbor. When I was a little girl, my childhood friend and I said that we would move to New York City when we were old enough. One morning, I packed my suitcase, called my aunt in New York, and hopped on the bus. I stayed in New York for almost a week. It was a breath of fresh air! Well, New

York's air is far from fresh, but you know what I mean. I felt like a weight was lifted off of my shoulders. The energy alone was inspiring! Everyone was on the move and had somewhere to go. I loved it; and since I dreamed of moving to New York as a kid, it was inevitable for it to happen soon. I went back to Baltimore so excited and confident.

A few weeks later, while driving through a storm on my way home, I heard a soft voice say to me, *"What are you doing? You're a star."* I heard it so clearly that it caused me to press my break and sit at the green light while the car behind me beeped its horn. I rushed home and sat on the floor in my empty house. I prayed and sat quietly; and the next thing you know, I was doing a vision board with actors, authors, houses, travel; any and everything that I wanted. Honestly, at that time I didn't realize these were things that I wanted; especially acting and writing. Although they were things that I did as a child, they had been so far from my current reality. I don't know what my future holds, but I know what I heard; and whatever it happens to be, I am a star in my own right.

Taking that break to New York was another life changing moment for me; and from that moment on, I traveled to New York often, sometimes for acting class, and other times, just to be inspired. Take moments for yourself to find yourself or to just be free. Learn something new, eat something new! You never know where one experience might take you. My one experience helped me to tap into my true self.

Skipping Play Time Is Not an Option

The more responsibilities we take on, the less time we have for ourselves. It's nothing wrong with having a full book of responsibilities, but just don't forget to have playtime. Children play and use their imagination all the time. Just because you're a teenager or college student, or a young adult who has school, work, and other activities, does not mean you should not have any focus on just being happy and having a good time. Once again, I have been guilty of this. I allowed myself to be an adult so early that I forgot how to just have a great time. Don't get me wrong, in my early stages of independence, I turned up a little bit, but it quickly got less important, because I didn't know how to balance a good time with being responsible. Hakuna Matata, honey. Hakuna Matata!

Like Nike Said...Just Do It!

When I say, *"Do not exist...Live,"* I mean that in so many ways. That means being bold and going after whatever it is you want. It means to stop procrastinating and finally make the next move. It means having a game plan. It means so many things, but what I want you to take from it is, take chances, because this life only comes around one time. The last thing you want to do is wait until you feel too old to do the things you should have just went for at an early age. It doesn't matter what other people think, as long as you are doing something positive and fulfilling- go for it! A lot of the times, we wait for the perfect moment to do something, but the truth is, there is never a perfect moment to do anything. That perfect moment may be at the worst point of your life. I discovered I really wanted to be an actress at a very low point in my life; right after the death of my dad. I wrote my first book at a very challenging stage in my life; I was pregnant with no money and unable to audition. Those times can be the best times for you to discover yourself and make a move that could possibly lead you to something greater. There may be moments of fear, but you have to press through it.

My six-year-old told me she wanted to be a model, so I signed her up for a local fashion show. She practiced at least twice a week at home in my living room. The day of the show, we were ready! We got to the venue and there were so many girls and designers, and just a lot of chaotic energy. I could see on her face that she was nervous, but she wouldn't say anything. She was chosen by four out of six designers to wear their clothes. Finally, it's time to hit the stage and Chloe'Rae is put at the front of the line. She said, "Wait, can I go last?" I didn't realize how afraid she was. I said, "No, Chlo, you have to go first." She said, "I'm scared. I don't want to do it." I tried to talk her out of her fear, but it didn't work. I am not going to lie, I was so upset with her! Not because she didn't want to walk, but because she didn't give it a try. I wanted her to be brave and just give it one try; but, I also had to remember that she was only six. It took my husband, mother, and grandmother to remind me of that, because my fire was burning! All I'm trying to say is, just do it! I've been in my daughter's position, especially as a kid, but I would rather fail and know if it is or is not for me rather than to never take that chance.

I think the best role models are those who are fruitfully and confidentially themselves. They bring light to the world.

-Meryl Streep
Actress

LESSON FIVE

Let It Shine! Let It Shine!

As a child, my favorite aunt, Hattie, used to sing *"This Little Light of Mine, I'm Gonna Let It Shine!"* That was our song. She would sit in my room, read my poems, and sing that song to me. I did not pay close attention to the words in that song until my late twenties while singing it to my daughters. Before, it was just a special song that I shared with a special person in my life, a song that was left in my heart to remember her by. I did not realize that she was planting a seed of confidence and a beam of light in my spirit. The meaning of this song is to shine bright even when there is shade and to let nothing come between you and your smile. To walk tall, smile bright, and speak with authority and grace. It means that you should be your own burst of sunshine. Even when the rain falls, your light should shine through. To shine bright, you need a few tools to keep you going.

Head Up, Shoulders Back…

Confidence is everything. Not just for people to see, but for you to feel inside. Even if you have to fake it 'til you make it. The older you get, the more insecurities you find in yourself. Television, social media, guys, friends, sometimes even your family can lower your self-esteem. But, here is the thing; it's called SELF-esteem. That means that no one or nothing should be able to distract you from how you feel about yourself. There will always be someone that's prettier, can dress better, has more money, blah blah blah…who cares sis!? Your focus should be on how beautiful you are when you wake up in the morning. How intelligent you are and that God has given you a purposeful gift. Every morning before school, my six-year-old says, "I look good, I feel good, and it's all good! I'm number one, baby! I love myself, I love myself, I love myself-self-self!" She learned this chant in Pre-K. I think it is so awesome, because she starts her day off feeling good about herself.

When I say, "fake it 'til you make it," I mean even if you are not feeling like yourself, or you don't feel pretty or smart, you can work yourself up to confidence. Or you can simply find things about yourself that make you feel good. When my is energy is low and I'm feeling like a fly on the wall, I sit down in a quiet place like the park, my office, or my favorite chair, and I write in my journal. I record how I'm feeling and what I can do to change it. I also write what I am grateful for and what I admire about myself. By the time I'm done, I'm feeling better about myself. Or I take a hot shower, put on my favorite lotion, give myself a facial and spray some perfume. Those are things that make me feel beautiful. I will choose my cutest outfit and stay away from wearing all dark colors. Sometimes it takes all of those things to see how great you are; and that's okay, you are human. You will not always feel pretty or smart, but the key is to remind yourself daily so that the chances of you forgetting are slim.

Confidence says a lot about who you are, and how people will treat you. I, personally, admire people who are confident, but silent. Meaning, they don't feel the need to brag and boast about who they are and what they have. Their actions and the way they carry themselves say a lot. They don't feel the need to prove to people how great they are; it shows through action.

There will be days when you have to smile even when you are having a hard day. You will have to put on your game face and your cutest outfit. It may sound cliché, but it's the truth. Sometimes it takes more than just saying, *"I look good."* You have to actually put yourself together to feel like something. Bottom line is, the confidence is key to a great personality.

Confidence, Not Arrogance

I truly believe that one should be full of them selves. As Oprah has said, "My cup should runneth over." Meaning, you should believe in yourself at the highest regard and you should give yourself credit for all of your achievements. You'd better catch this drip! Now, don't get it twisted, there is a difference in confidence and arrogance. When you are consistently talking about yourself, or you think you are just downright better than the next guy, or in our case, next girl; that can be a problem, simply because no one likes to be around a person who thinks they are better than everyone. Again, it's okay to hold yourself at a standard and high regard, but we are not interested in being around someone who never thinks they are wrong or only cares about what they have to say and so on.

Walking Tall

During my modeling years as a little girl, there were a few things I learned from modeling instructors. Head up, shoulders back! Walk like you own it! There were times I forgot what "head up and shoulders back" meant. It means to walk in the room shining with confidence and ready for whatever. Remember the salon I spoke about earlier? Well, at that time the owner inspired me. She would walk in that salon every day like, *"This is mine! I own this!"* And, I loved it! I was going through a low time in my life at that time, but her presence reminded me that I am a queen who deserves a seat at whatever table I choose to sit at. Regardless of what you are going through, never let people see you sweat! Walk tall, baby sister, and show them that, *"I deserve to be here!"* Put a smile on your face and speak clear with confidence and intelligence, because your presentation will take you a long way. Even if you are having the worst day ever, you remember that you may have to put on a show just to get through; and believe me you would not be the first.

Every Caterpillar Becomes a Butterfly and...

...Every planted seed will grow if watered properly. One of my favorite sayings is, *"When I step out of this cocoon and spread my beautiful wings...!"* Before a butterfly becomes a butterfly, it goes through a few transitions that will allow the butterfly to mature and get its wings to fly away. First, the butterfly is born into a caterpillar. It crawls around on the ground as it takes time to understand where it is, how to eat and learn its surroundings. After reaching its limit on the ground, it prepares a cocoon for it to nest in. The cocoon is a covering that hangs from a branch or something high. No one can see what is going on in that cocoon, but the caterpillar. He is in there going through transition and allowing his change to occur. When it is his time, he will break out of the cocoon with a set of wings and fly away, leaving the cocoon to decompose.

I love this metaphor, because it's real life! Not just for the caterpillar, but for people! We have to crawl before we walk, and we have to walk before we soar. You have to understand where you are before you can transition into something greater. Go through all of your changes, learn more and more about yourself every day. Learn more and more about life every day; and when it is time for you to transition to your next phase, you will be ready to pursue your next level. Some can say that they were born with a legacy built and a million dollars in the bank. But, for the rest of us; we have to work for it and learn more about ourselves, what we want, and how to get it. Some have spent years in their cocoon before flourishing. Me... I am still in my cocoon. A year ago, I may not have been fine with that, because I didn't fully understand what it meant to be in a cocoon. I just thought I was being unrecognized and no one saw my talent. However, I was not ready for people to fully see my potential, because I still had a lot of growing to do. And, that is okay! It's okay to be hidden, because it gives you time to fully create a better you! Just think about when those wings stretch out and those bright beautiful colors wave across the sky! It will all be worth the wait.

Steve Harvey is one of my media mentors. He is my uncle in my head. I call him Uncle Steve! You will probably hear about a few aunts and uncles, sisters, and brothers in this book that I have never met! Girl, it's all in my head! But, anyway, I have been following Uncle Steve for years now, as he has transitioned from comedy to a television host, to radio host, and now author and motivational speaker. I watch Youtube videos daily for inspiration; and in one of the videos I was watching, Uncle Steve was the keynote speaker for Pastor TD Jakes a few years back. One thing that stuck to me was his analogy of seeds and how they grow. Seeds are planted in the ground and they have to be covered with dirt. After the dirt is put down, they need water to be nourished and to grow. This is the same for your life. We cannot expect to grow and get through life without challenges and detours. If God has put something in you and has a plan for your life, you will get there. However, it's not that easy; because there will be a few interruptions to throw you off your game, but it's not for you to quit. It's for you to learn from it, build your character, and grow anyway. Your job is to figure out how to get through it and move on with the plan. Great opportunities may come while you are on your journey. Those things may curb your vision a little; and it may look like it's better than what was there before. That is when you silence yourself to make sure you are making the right decision. Just remember that His plan will always be His plan. It's up to you to continue growing.

Be That Breath of Fresh Air

Let me start by saying this…There is nothing wrong with being different! We watch reality shows and hop on Instagram and want to be like the next chick. No ma'am! Be a breath of fresh air; show us something we haven't seen before. If you are doing something similar to someone else, tweak it and make it your own; be authentic. DON'T BE FAKE! In 2009, I did a modeling competition in DC for a magazine. During the casting process, I had to walk in dressed in a bathing suit. I smiled and was just being my usual "around the way girl with a dash of class" self. I wore my natural hair bone straight with a razor cut shag and bangs. When I walked in, the judges all seemed very tense, until I stood in front of them. After they interviewed me, one lady said, "Is that your real hair?"

I answered with a smile, "Yes."

The lady next to her said, "You have been a breath of fresh air."

"Thank you," I said, as I exited.

On my way out, the assistant said, "You were the only girl that smiled and didn't look like a Barbie doll."

Of course, I took that as a compliment. People want to see *you*. Now, if you are just ratchet-ratchet-ratchet, then you need to make some changes, ASAP! All I'm saying is, be yourself and allow people to enjoy being in your presence.

Never Dim Your High Beams

There has been plenty of times in the past when I have put my high beams on low to accommodate someone else's feelings, but the moment I realize that it was diminishing my character, I stopped! It's not cute; and it makes you look weak! No one can shade your shine unless you let them. I mean, seriously, it took me a long time to realize how bad it was making me look. Then one day, I said to myself, *"Girl stand up for yourself! She's jealous of you anyway!"* One particular time, I went to my old neighborhood to visit some friends and I jokingly called one of them ignorant. One of my guy friends said, "Do you know what ignorant means?" And for some stupid reason, I told him no. I'm shaking my head as I type, because what in this world would have changed if I would have just shut his whole life down and said, " Yes, ignorant means without knowledge of or unknowing; however sometimes we use it in a jokingly manner such as 'stupidity or rudeness'". Then, I would have watched him pick his face up off the ground. Instead, I chose to hide under a rock and look stupid. Never again! People will only make you feel the way you allow them to, so girl, stop it at the door!

Your light should shine bright; and if they are blinded, then tell them to buy some expensive shades, because you are not here for it!

Give Me the Ball and Watch What I Do with It

When I was a little girl, there was a movie called "*Hardball*." Before the movie dropped, a video came out with a few of my favorite rappers. I was over the top obsessed with Lil Bow Wow, who was one of the rappers, and I remember, in the video, when he got up to the plate to hit the baseball, Jermaine Dupri says, "Give me the ball and watch what I do wit it." That saying has stuck with me ever since. It means that when my moment comes, I'm going to shine.

After all of your preparing and mastering, you just want somebody to notice you. This subject has been the most challenging in my life. The moment I decided to pursue acting as a career, I just wanted to be noticed. Scratch that...All through my adolescence, I felt like I was unnoticed, but once I fell in love with acting, being noticed became my main goal. I just wanted the gold. I did not care about anything else; I just wanted to be noticed. I even tried to skip a few steps to make it happen, but it wasn't working out for me, so I took a step back to see what I needed to do to pursue this dream. I took classes and got in a few local projects. I had to consistently prove myself. I often heard how great of an actor I was. Finally, I flew to LA to audition for a big-time director. He had an open call. I got to the open call an hour early and was still, like, the hundredth person in line. I stood in line for over eight hours with five-inch heels on, and I refused to take them off. My prayer on the plane was, *"God I don't care about what happens at this audition, I just want them to know my name."* After hours of standing in this line, they were about to shut the auditions down and move to another location because they went over their time. I begged them to let me audition, because I had been there since nine o'clock that morning, and it was now going on eight o'clock at night. My plane was scheduled to leave in three hours. They brought me in and let me audition. While performing my piece, I noticed them passing around my head shot and whispering to each other. When I was done, I said, "Thank you," and I walked off of the stage. As I begin to exit, the director stopped the auditions and called my name. Literally, my heart skipped a beat. He called me over to the casting table and asked me why hadn't I moved to LA. At that time, I actually had plans to move. He then said, "We will be calling you." I nodded my head and said, "Thank you," again. I left the audition in tears. I drove to Malibu and sat on the beach and cried. I know it's a little dramatic, but it's the truth. I did get the call, but I didn't make it past the second audition process. I even had a few chances to meet with that director afterward.

I decided shortly after that I didn't want to wait for people to notice me; I would get up in their faces. I did that by writing my own material. No one will believe how great you are until you show them. My first book was my proof to myself that I can knock it out the park.

Party or Build an Empire

Big brother Diddy says, "Lock In!" That means focus. If you have a goal to reach, you have to focus to get it completed. If hanging out with your girls or your boyfriend is more important, then it's really not that important to you. I have missed a number of events because I knew that if I broke my focus, I may not get that momentum back. Besides that, partying is not that important. You better secure the bag! Thou shalt not put anything before it! Becoming great takes a lot of sacrifice and balance. That word still scares me 'til this day! Balance. I am a mother of two, and a wife with an entrepreneurial attitude and big dreams, so balance is not easy! So, if I have to make it happen (which can be very hard), then so can you! You better focus on what is essential in your life. You can't have a great time if your life isn't in order or you're broke. You will not pursue your dreams if you find partying and spending money to be more important.

Underestimate Me. I Like It!

I think that I have done a great job with allowing people to underestimate me. I hit them with a *boom*!

"Wow, you wrote a book?"

"Um, yes, I did; while you thought I had nothing going on."

Being underestimated can be used to your advantage. There will be times when you tell your dreams to people and they will not flinch; no words and no actions. They will act like you never said a word. Usually, that's their way of throwing it under the rug or not believing in it. Or they are simply haters and you should probably never, ever tell them anything else. DON'T BELIEVE ME JUST WATCH. Do not let it discourage you; just smile and keep it moving. The reactions you receive should not diminish your dream.

As you make decisions on life and what you want to do, just know that there will be dirt thrown and everyone will not agree with your dream. Here's the thing…it's none of their business anyway! They have no power over if you win or lose! That is between you and God, that's it. One of three things can happen… Your dream will become a reality and you will get exactly what you asked for; you may fail once, twice, maybe three times; or you come to a conclusion that this isn't working out and you go another route. None of those things need approval from someone else. Unless you need a loan; but that's another story. Keep going until you hear them say, *"I remember when she told me about that."* Just give them the side eye and a smile.

As a woman, we have to shout, play the politics and make sure we do what we gotta do so we're not shut out. If you don't pipe up, you'll end up with something you're not proud of.

-Lena Waithe

"Never go through life trying to be someone else. God made you uniquely you!"

- Tamara Housley
Actress and Co-Host of "The Real"

LESSON SIX

I Am A Woman First

I don't care what you decide to do with your life, just do it with integrity and have a plan. Have morals and good character. Just remember that people will always remember the crazy side of you and how wild you used to be. We all have a past that we need to grow from. So, just do your best at being the best you. Do not forget that, above all, you are a woman first!

Show Class Not...I'm Sure You Know the Rest

The subtitle is not necessarily literal, but it is. I said to myself, *"This is a touchy subject."* To be honest, I don't care, because I strongly believe that a woman can be successful without selling her soul or her goodies. However, to each his own. Right now, we live in a culture filled with social media models and reality television. It gives the illusion that this is what you need to do, and this is how you have to be if you want to be seen and heard. That is not always the case. You may not have a popcorn career; meaning an overnight success, but at least you can say it took a lot more than your good looks to make it happen. I'm not going to lie…I have indulged in reality television every once in a while, but, I do not mirror some of what I have seen. I am not bashing any one, but, you should not have to fight, disrespect yourself or others to be seen or successful. Like I said, this is a touchy subject! Yes, sometimes you have to set a chick straight, but should you devalue yourself to do so? There are a few that have made great success from social media and reality television that I can honestly say, "Yo, I really like how she moves. Her hustle is real." And some are just being themselves. Just don't be extra just to get extra. That is all I am saying.

In my early 20's I received an opportunity to be in a swimsuit competition. From there, I signed to an agent who I later found out was not the best move for me; but in my mind, *I had an agent*. Since I was too short to do runway (which was my first passion), I thought vixen modeling would get me to the next level in my career path. I had a photo shoot with my agent, and most of those photos were okay, but I also had a few that were not flattering. I soon decided that this was not the way I wanted to go. I wanted to be known for so much more. I am saying all of this to say that, yes, you will make decisions that you later realize were not the best, but try to make them before you are too deep in.

If you are a young girl reading this book, I want you to know that there are plenty of great examples of what independent and beautiful women look like. They are business- women, wives and mothers, even young girls in their teens. Some came from wealthy homes and some are straight out of the hood. These women make boss moves every day. Do not believe that you have to degrade yourself in any way to gain success. Getting "likes" is not where the world began, and it is definitely not where the world ends.

Self-Awareness and Self Worth

You have to know that you, and you alone, are enough! Do not get so wrapped up in things that really don't matter. Your followers do not define you or bring you value. Your intelligence, confidence, and how hard you are willing to grind is all that matters. You need to know that! We get so caught up in who likes us on social media that we get distracted with the real world. Stop spending so much time trying to mirror what you see everyone else doing and focus on who you are becoming.

Be aware of who you are; if not, you will get lost in trying to imitate what you see. Yes, she takes great pictures and she slays every look, her Prada bag is gorgeous and so is those Yves Saint Laurent stilettos, but you don't know what she did to get those things - good or bad. Was it blood, sweat, and tears; or did she sell the "cookies?" Either way, that's not your business. Just focus on how you can get it; and feel good about it later.

Taking time for yourself and understanding who you are is self-awareness. Take care of you first! That is how you grow your self-worth. You are not going to allow other people to treat you any less than you treat yourself if you already know how you want to be treated. If you have high expectations for how you treat yourself, you should not lower them for other people. We teach people how to treat us by how we treat ourselves. It took a very long time for me to learn my self-worth. I put on the mask of knowing exactly who I was and what my worth was, but I was still lost trying to figure myself out. I wouldn't stand up for myself, and there was a time where my husband and I had split. We have been together since high school, but we have had a few break ups, and during those times, I did a little dating or whatever. I cringe at how I allowed myself to be treated. I set a standard for myself, but I didn't stick to it, and it showed in how I felt. Even before I married my husband, there were things that I put up with that I would not put up with now. You have to be careful with how you allow people to see you or treat you, because if not, it will be an invitation for them to treat you however they want.

After the birth of Harley, my youngest, I had an emotional breakdown. Most would say it was postpartum depression, but to be honest, I was dealing with it on and off for a long time - well before Harley was thought of. At that time, Harley was about four months old and I was completely exhausted and overwhelmed. This may not resonate with you in the form of parenting; however, these same feelings will take place with school and becoming an independent adult. One day, I found myself in the kitchen with my mother and husband. I was crying my little heart out as I expressed to them what I was going through. I felt like nothing in my life was getting accomplished. I felt smothered by responsibilities, and I was not motivated to do anything that I love because I couldn't find the time or balance to do so.

After I had this breakdown, I got dressed and went to a job that I absolutely hated. I sat in a quiet booth and pulled out a journal that I had recently purchased from Barnes and Nobles. It became my "self-help journal." I used it to do what I call an emotional dump. I wrote down exactly how I was feeling and none of it looked good to me. Then, I wrote what I could do to feel better. Then, I wrote down all of the things that made me happy and what I was grateful for. Finally, I wrote paragraphs about what I did not like about myself and what I would do to change them. During this writing process, I begin to find relief. All of those feelings of hopelessness were fading away because I searched deep down in myself to find the light. I realized that I have the power to make these changes, but it would start with my mind first.

I would strongly suggest that you do the same. Start here! This will hold you accountable for your actions and will help you release your self-esteem issues little by little.

Self-Help Journal

What Does Self-Esteem Mean to You?
(Ask yourself this question.)

What Makes Me Happy?

____

____

____

____

How Do I Feel Right Now?

____

____

____

____

What Do I Dislike About Myself?

How Can I Change These Things?

I Am Grateful For…

This is just a starter kit, but a daily journal would be great!

All Attention Isn't Good Attention…

…Nor is it all good intentions. As people, we all desire some attention; some more than others. It can be a guy, an opportunity, or a "friend". Sometimes we just want to be seen and acknowledged by others. Believe it or not it is natural to receive some kind of validation. You should not make getting attention or receiving validation a mission in your life. It will make you absolutely insane if you do not receive it. If you do make attention and validation your mission you will spend a lot of time trying to be someone you are not. Obviously, you feel that who you are is not good enough or you wouldn't have to work so hard. Stay true.

Back to those intentions…Watch out for people and situations that may not be right for you. There may be a guy that you are interested in that finally says hello. He may even ask you out. In your eyes he is perfect. Handsome, well-dressed, and a good head on his shoulders, but after spending some time with him you realize all he wanted was "your gold mine;" and since you are not willing to give it away, he skips out. Or maybe there is a girl in your school who wants to become friends, but you later realize that she only wanted to get close to you to tear you down. Maybe there is an opportunity that you have been waiting for that will bring you more money. When you finally get started you realize that you are working sixteen hours, five days straight, and have no time to rest or enjoy your life. It may not look as good anymore. These are just examples of how you can get something that you want and it is not exactly what you need.

Girl! What Are You Wearing?

Okay, so I am not telling you to go out and spend all of your money on clothes, but I am saying that you should always look presentable. I will be the first to say, yes, I have my days! We all do! But, if my hair is not pressed, it is in my natural curls or pulled back into my trusty bun! Whatever the case may be, the look always works together. The way you dress is a mirror of who you are and how you feel. Sometimes how you feel is not everyone's business. Sometimes, you have to get up and put on your highest heels, your cutest flats, or a dope pair of sneakers. During my years in high school, I definitely allowed how I felt to show up in my wardrobe. My first year of high school, I made sure everything matched and looked good. I was ready to walk the halls. Even if I didn't have a lot of money I still did my best at being presentable. Close to the end of the year, I went through a deep depression that no one knew about. It carried into the tenth grade. I was dealing with a lot at home with my parents and I didn't feel good about myself. I started wearing big t-shirts and my hair was all over my head some days. I honestly felt like, *what's the point of dressing up? One day I won't be here*. I know that is a little extreme, but that is how I felt. My mood changed all of the time. Some days, I felt great, other days I didn't, and my clothes showed it. You will not always feel great about yourself and you may not always have the best clothes, but even if you have one pair of jeans, two pairs of shoes, and a few blouses, take care of what you have and do your best at wearing it well until you can do better.

Everyone has their own style; but, as women, I truly believe there are a few essential pieces we need in our closet. Cami's, white and black t-shirts, a pair of black heels and/or flats, a nice pair of fitted jeans, a little black dress, a blazer, a pair of trousers, leggings, a cute pair of sneakers, and don't forget graphic tees. A jean jacket and a cute summer dress couldn't hurt either. In my eyes, these are essentials, because you can do so much with them and switch them up in different ways. For example, you may have an interview after school for a clothing store, but you don't have time to go home and change. Well, if you wear your fitted t-shirt and jeans to school, you can carry your blazer with you to wear to the interview. Or if you are out running errands and your girlfriends want to meet up for a quick get-together, but you have on a pair of leggings some sneakers and a cami, you can quickly go home and change your shoes and layer with a cute jacket. Or you can be like me and have an extra pair of everything in the trunk (sometimes, not always). Don't judge me!

This may not be your "look" at all. I switch up my look all of the time. It's boring to dress the same every day. But, whatever your look is, choose your essentials and put some color in the mix every once in a while. You could always create a look book of your favorite looks. I use Pinterest for everything that my little heart desires. I also look through magazines for inspiration. If you have a look book of ideas and fashion you will have a guide when you are shopping or organizing your closet.

If there are things in your closet that you hate or you do not plan on wearing again throw it out or give it away! There is no reason to build up clutter with pieces that do not work for you. I recently had this conversation with my husband. I hate doing laundry. Not necessarily the washing and drying, but the folding! OMG, it drives me insane! A few days ago, I was doing laundry and I realized that we have a lot of irrelevant pieces. Dingy t-shirts, leggings that were torn, some stuff had stains and looked old. Those were the "around the house clean up and play" clothes. But, how many "around the house clean up and play" clothes do you need? I started throwing them away. My husband got in his feelings, but I didn't care. There is no need for twenty white dingy t-shirts. Take inventory and get rid of the mess.

It's not always a thing about making a good impression on others; make a good impression on yourself. You deserve to feel good and look good.

Homework! I want you to go on Pinterest and download the app. Type in, "girl or women fashion." Get more specific if you would like. If you rock sneakers or stilettos, rocker chic, or boho chic, find what works for you. Check out your body shape and make sure that the looks you pick out works with your body shape. Are you busty, curvy, slim, thick on top and bottom? Start a look book. Then look in your closet and see if you have anything in your closet that you can put together to make those looks. Don't start throwing all of your clothes away. If there are things that don't work for you, just wing them off as you buy new pieces. The last thing you want to do is empty your closet on impulse.

Take Care of Yourself First

There is nothing wrong with feeling like a woman. We get our hair done, our nails done, facials, wax, we shop, eat, and entertain. All of these things are great, so take care of yourself, but don't break your bank account to do so. If you do not make enough money to pamper yourself once a week, then space it out. Hair this week, nails next week or once a month. Between my two girls, my husband, and work, it can be really difficult for me to have some time alone, because I am on high demand to everybody and everything else…even the dog! I am STILL learning balance; and, in a way, I still suck at it.

Sometimes, I have to steal my own time. Right now, it is five o'clock in the morning and I am up talking to you! Do my husband and children look at me crazy sometimes? Yes. Yes they do. But, some days, I have to grab my gym bag, put on my shades and roll. You cannot give all of you to everyone else and leave just a small percentage for yourself. Believe me, it is dangerous. So, before you are my age with children, a man, blah blah blah…Get in tune with taking care of yourself now.

I didn't pamper myself a lot in my younger years, because I didn't see my mother put a lot of time into pampering herself. She was always helping this person and that person or caring for us and working. She never really took time for herself. As a matter of fact, one year I sent her to get a massage for her birthday and she rushed it. Her exact words were, "How long will this take? I have something to do." Like really, Ma!? It's a massage…relax! She was so in tune with being too busy that she didn't know how to sit still and be pampered.

School will be exhausting. Then, add studying, your job, family, the list goes on. But, at some moment, I want you to cut yourself off from all of that, even if it takes you telling a small fib to get a moment to yourself.

Now, if you are in high school reading this book, I don't mean tell your parents you are going to the library, but, you end up at a party or your boyfriend's house. I tried it and believe me the consequences were not cute at all, quite embarrassing, actually. I am saying that if you are exhausted and just need a second, and the only way to take a walk is to say you're going to the store, then go for it; but, please be back at a decent hour, and don't make this an everyday thing (the fibs, I mean).

For years, I wouldn't go to a hair salon because I could do my own hair, but it feels so much better when someone else does it. This year, I am starting a new practice for myself called, Self-Love Weekend. During my self-love weekend, I do things that I love - whatever that may be. Going shopping, painting, going to a play, even getting a hotel room and just writing all day. Whatever makes me happy. This is my way of revitalizing myself and preserving energy for everyone and everything else. Take time to just be a girl, and thank me later.

Last, but not least, take care of your body. I know you've heard it before, but your body really is your temple. What goes in it will show up in your day to day performance and your physical features. Believe me I know!

Yes, I work out and I eat pretty good, but at the same time, I love to eat. I am a true foodie and I will try almost anything. I grew up in West Baltimore where I could get a chicken box (four chicken wings and fries to be exact) and a cheesesteak on every corner. If I want a crab cake or whatever, I will get it. But, at the same time, it's not an everyday thing. And, my body tells me when it's not used to something. I get sluggish and my face gets fuller. On the flip side, there have been days without a full meal and water, just because I was too wrapped up in my day to eat! That is ridiculous, and it sounds even worse coming out of my mouth. I would feel and look terrible. Try to make a meal plan for yourself and re-evaluate what you're eating. Try to stay active on the regular, even if it is taking a walk. Good sleep will change your attitude; nobody likes a demon in the morning.

Yeah, I Got an Attitude...And?

"It's not that bad...Smile." Ugh! A guy's favorite pick up line. Will someone please remind them that it does not work!? My resting face looks like I could be the meanest chick in the world, but that's not the case. There are times when I try to look more pleasant so that others will know that I am approachable. From a teenager to adulthood, I not only had a resting face, but at times I would say whatever came to my mind. Nothing has gotten me in trouble more than my mouth. My attitude caused me to have bad relationships in my work place and even lose some jobs. I was always good at my jobs, but I had a problem with being told what to do. That alone is a big problem…period. Word from the wise: You have to know how to follow before you can lead. Yes, I was dealing with a lot internally, but in public is not the best place to show off your personal issues. When working with people you want them to be comfortable around you, not unsure of what attitude they will get today. At the end of the day, your attitude will affect your coins and your relationships with other people; and both of those go a long way. So, even if your coworker or teacher is getting on your last nerves and you want to give her a piece of your mind, just smile and give it to her in the most pleasant way possible.

Recently, I found myself WAY off of the cliff. I allowed a co-worker to get me so far up in my feelings. I started yelling at them over the phone. When I got off of the phone, I was angrier with myself than the situation. I had allowed myself to go back to a temperament that I have worked very hard to free myself from. When you check someone with grace, it is so much more satisfying than when you do it with a loud mouth and screaming. Keep your cool and keep your power. What has helped me in situations, such as heated phone calls or disagreements, is preparing myself mentally before it happens. I try to focus on the solution to the situation. Therefore, during the conversation, I'm not entering with a defensive objective. The whole idea should be to come to a solution after sharing your concerns.

Remember this...you don't always have to show how much you know or how smart you are. In some cases, the best thing to do is sit back and listen. And, in other cases, there may be an immediate need for your ideas or interpretation. Of course, you should work to the best of your ability, but never know so much that there is nothing you can learn. There is always something new to learn even if it does not align with what you are doing right now. You never know where life will take you. That skill may be needed in your future. Ask questions. Good leaders love to work with people who are interested in learning more, and sometimes the more you learn, the less they have to do. But, if you come across a person that doesn't want to teach you something that you are interested in learning, just watch or learn from someone who is willing to teach you.

Keep Your Grass Cut Low

Have you ever heard the saying, "*Keep your grass cut low so that you can see the snakes?*" Every time I had a new group of friends, my mother used to find at least one out of the bunch and she would say, "Baby, she ain't your friend. She don't mean you no good." She would say it so much that it got on my nerves. For years, I believed that my mother didn't want me to have friends. It wasn't until I became an adult that I realized she was right most of the time.

There is no such thing as "fr-enemy". We're either friends, or we're not. I grew up as the only girl on the block. The guys in my neighborhood kept me grounded, they were my friends and a lot of the time, if I fought someone, it was one of them. As I got older, I yearned for girlfriends, because the guys didn't play dress up and do all of the girly things that I had to do alone. We played basketball on Hoop City, Nintendo 64, and tag. So, the moment I got girlfriends, I tried to hold on to them; even if it meant being naïve. There was always one who said I thought that I was cute, rolled her eyes every chance she got, or would even try to embarrass me with a loud outburst. When a person shows you that they really don't deal with you, believe them. Don't try to be their friend or make them like you…it is what it is. They could have better clothes and more money, but it will be something about you that they will hate on. So, when you see the shade, just get from under it.

We all have this thing of "being accepted" and validated. Stop trying to get in the circle and build your own. Not just with friends, but in life. I spent a lot of time in my life wanting to be accepted and caring about being liked. Especially, by those who had a serious dislike for me. I spent so much of my energy trying to please and be nice to people that I lost my self-respect and respect from others. You cannot please everyone. I believe it was TD Jakes who said, "The disease to please will wreak havoc on your life". This statement is so true! Everyone will not love you. Some will just hate the fact that you smiled today. That's not your problem; that is theirs. Stop asking for everyone's permission to be great! Stop showing off to be seen. If people cannot see how uniquely made you are, then they are not meant to be in your company.

On the flip side of that, there may be a friend who is playing friend. Yes, I said it. She is fake and phony, so watch her! Sometimes people want to get close to you just so they can have access to what you have. The moment they get a chance to switch up or tell your business, they will. That brings me to my next point. Stop telling everybody your business! Girl, seriously! I had to learn that the hard way. I still regret telling some of my closest friends my business, because you just don't know if they will use it against you one day. Now, I'm not saying that you shouldn't trust anyone, but you should be very selective of who you trust. Furthermore, when a person knows too much about you, it gives them a window to always give their opinion without permission. Or, they get comfortable and have no protocol on how they treat you.

I will use a few examples of a shady friend:

1. You are in a committed relationship with a great guy, but your friend tries to hook you up with someone. Shady!

2. You tell her a secret and hear it from someone else. Shady!

3. You know that dress is fitting all kinds of wrong and she allows you to go out looking all kinds of

wrong. You need to leave her where she stands! Shady!

4. You have positive vibes; maybe something great is going on in your life and she constantly finds something wrong. She is a hater! Shady!
5. She tries to embarrass you in front of other people. Shady!
6. Every time you invite her to an event, she can't make it. Dispose of her! Shady!
7. You are going through something and she is there every step of the way, but the moment you get back on top, the shade is thrown. Or, just the opposite... when you're on top she is there until you fall short. Shady! Shady! Shady! Consistency is key, my love.

There is a whole list of shady examples. I could certainly go on forever, but you get the picture.

Sometimes, it takes years to see someone's shade towards you. Don't be naïve sweetheart. She or he has shown you who she or he is; live with it and move on.

It's always the people that know the least about you that want to judge you the most.
-Kylie Jenner

Look at people for an example, but then, make sure to do things yourself with positive people.
-Queen Latifah
Singer, Actress, Rapper, Producer

LESSON SEVEN

Girl, You Have Issues
Personal Growth & Development

The Past is The Past...Now Let's Get It

Your past does not define you. This is life. You will make a million mistakes, but that does not mean you can't come back from them. Your mistakes do not define who you are or who you will be. However, some mistakes can be more damaging than others and some decisions can be thought through a little more.

I spent a lot of my time thinking about the mistakes I made and how I could have done things differently. I held things over my head for years; losing sleep thinking about what I should have said to someone or how I made myself look stupid. Wallowing in shoulda, coulda, woulda's is nothing but a headache. It does not change your past, but it can damage your future. The best thing about your past mistakes is that you can learn from them and make them up in the future.

The older you get, the more mistakes you will make. So, try to see them as experiences and not regrets. My father used to say that he has no regrets in his life, because everything is a learning experience. Now the truth is, we all have a regret somewhere, but I understood what he was saying. If you see every experience as a learning experience, then, of course, there are no regrets. That is what life is about. It's a path of learning tools that will prepare you for your next chapter and the chapter after that. Each tool will be needed somewhere in your future, good and bad. The worst you go through, the greater the lesson. I know that sounds harsh, but I truly believe this. Just because something bad happens in your life, doesn't mean that it will be there forever; especially if you pay attention to the lesson. That's the advantage that we all have. The lesson is what changes things.

God has always revealed to me His reasons for putting me through whatever it was He put me through. Each and every single time something amazing happens, He gives me visions of all the steps and trials He put me through to get me to where I am. And, then, it all begins to make sense. I would cry and scream, "Why me, God? Why me?" Not realizing that I had to have a little dirt thrown on me to grow to my next level.

Before I wrote my first book, my focus was on acting and acting only. I began to take my career very serious. I was ripping and running; I moved to New York, moved back home, and traveled to LA for auditions. My head was all over the place. All I knew was that I wanted to act, but I could not sit still long enough to know what to do. So, God sat me still. In 2010, I moved back from New York and planned to move to LA the following year. In August of 2010, I found out I was pregnant with my daughter. I'm going to be honest with you, because otherwise I would be a fake. But, I was devastated and terrified! I wasn't ready to be someone's mother and neither was my boyfriend. We had unresolved issues and I wanted to just focus on my career and be free from distractions. Clearly, God had other plans. After a few months, I finally became at peace with being a mother, and I was overjoyed; but, the one thing that was scary for me was how I would continue my path to become an actress? Rewinding back to a few months before August, I wrote a script for a drama series called, *"Misunderstanding".* Shortly after, things went bad and we stopped filming. I became so obsessed with the production of this script. Fast forwarding back to my pregnancy; when I finally got to my fifth month, I was too big to audition. I had people asking me, "What about my career?" or "You can't have a baby in Hollywood." First of all, big sister Taraji did it all on her own! Auntie Niecy Nash did it, too, and I'm sure there are a few more brave Queens on the list who had to put their babies on their backs! So, mind your business and watch a real "G" do this! Now that I got that little rant out of the way…I sat for weeks trying to figure out what I could do to keep myself inspired and productive. (Notice I said *productive* and not *busy.* We will discuss this later.) So, I decided to turn my screenplay into a novel called "*Easily Enticed.*"

Fast forward to 2013. I finally released my book. August 7, 2013 to be exact. I went through so much during those years, but I never stopped writing. One day, my boyfriend and I were driving to Philadelphia to sell some books and God gave me a flash of visions. They were all of my trials and tough situations that lead up to that point. He also showed me what my future would have been if I had moved to LA at that time. I started to cry, because I realize that every single situation had prepared me for this one stepping-stone towards my future. If I had never gotten pregnant with my daughter, I would have not only missed out on the biggest blessing of my life, but I would have moved to LA with all of my craziness and lack of knowledge. I would have never sat down to write a novel. This full chapter of my life would be missing; and I couldn't imagine life without my girls. My life would have fallen apart, because I wasn't ready. Even though I was in some challenging situations, it taught me patience and resilience.

If every millionaire or billionaire in this world let their past define them, they would not be who they are today. Steve Harvey and Oprah Winfrey both agree that you have to fail over and over again to perfect and grow. Without mistakes you will never figure out how to get life right, and even then, you will make more mistakes.

NO? Well, What Does That Mean Exactly?

One thing that I have learned from my spiritual leaders is that no does not always mean no. Sometimes, it means *not right now.* If you are anything like me, 'not right now" sounds just like "no". Thank God that is not always the case. You don't have to accept a no, but "not right now" may work out in your favor. That just means that you have more time to prepare in whatever way you need to. Don't lose focus and don't quit, just continue to prepare. My husband is the most cautious, most patient person when it comes to life situations. And, to be honest, I absolutely hate it! I've heard "give it some time" and "hold up" so many times that it is engraved in my brain. Sometimes, it's just dreadful to hear, but, other times, it makes more sense for me to hold things off just in case something different comes through or I need to gather more wisdom before moving forward.

Never take no as the final answer. You don't have to protest to the person who told you no, just prove to them why they should have said yes. Which means that enough hard work should have been done to prove your "yes." *No* has been a hard word for me to swallow in the past. I would get all in my head. I would start doubting myself. That can be the worst thing that you do, because it becomes a trickling effect. Now, you are downing yourself and finding every negative thing to complain about.

Never Be Afraid to Ask

Have you ever wanted something and got the opportunity to possibly receive it, but you were just too afraid to ask? I have done this so many times and each time I would regret not speaking up. Recently, I had a conversation with a well-known actress and after the conversation, I failed to give her my contact information just in case any of my services were needed. It was done subconsciously; and I didn't realize it until I got home. I was so upset with myself. That was an opportunity for my information to be passed along and my talents to be used. With that said, be ready! People cannot read your mind, and scared money don't make money. When I was a little girl, I was scared to speak up, even though I knew I could do something better than the next person. This habit carried on into early adulthood. I was scared to take on leadership roles, although, I knew I was right for the job. You can't be afraid to be great. You will miss out and limit yourself. My mother used to say, "The worst thing they could say is 'no,' and then you figure out what to do with that." Yes, some people can be intimidating, but, stand your ground, be confident in yourself, and remember that people are people - they are no different than you. Those are words from my O.G, Wendy Williams- my mommy.

Although, I have had a few hits and misses, I have taken advantage of most of my opportunities. When you realized that nothing is changing and you need results, you will speak up. Ask for what you want and be ready to receive it.

Listen to God. He's the Man in Charge

I don't know who your higher being may be - God, the universe, whatever floats your boat. God is my inner being and my universe, who manifests all that I ask for. When I am lost and confused about life decisions, I get crazy, and then I get still. I used to ask this person and that person for their opinion. Sometimes I may get some good advice, but I still take some quiet time to talk to God or just be quiet enough to listen. I ask questions and I wait for the answer; although sometimes, the answer comes much later. I go to the source, because people are going to give you all types of opinions; and that's exactly what they are. It's an opinion. Which means they are basing the answer off of what they would do. That's not always going to work for you. You are not them. If you need answers, go to your source or your inner being. That way, you will not have to decide on who has the best opinion.

Do You Boo! Do You!

When I was in high school, my, now, mother-in-law, used to lecture me all of the time; and the main topic was, "Do you!". I did not really understand until life got really real and I was willingly giving all of me to my relationship and leaving myself a little empty. I thought she was trying to keep me away from her son! "Do you" means to put no one else before your needs. No one! Yes, it may sound a little selfish, and yes, you should be selfless at times, but if you don't get yourself right, you cannot help anyone else. Ms. Maya Angelou says to "Love yourself first; and if a naked person is willing to give you a shirt, then you should not trust them." As women, we spend a lot of time trying to help others. Especially, our boyfriends, family and sometimes our closest girlfriends. You cannot fix them; and do not spend so much time trying to. Time will pass, and you will realize that you have not watered your own seeds. Nourish your own mind, body, soul, and finances before you try to nourish someone else. People will use you for whatever they can use you for. In the mean time you have been used to capacity and still try to give. When they are done with you, they will find someone else to use up.

If the Help Is Not There, Google It! Better Yet, Read A Book!

The most successful people in this world take time to sit back, relax, and read a book. You may not be an avid reader as I am. It took a lot of growth and maturity for me to become a reader; but more than anything, it was my hunger for the knowledge that I was not getting elsewhere. Although I have the bloodline of a true hustler, I did not grow up around millionaires or business owners. In order for me to learn the mind of a millionaire, I had to read about it, or Youtube myself crazy. There is a book out there for everything you want or need to know. Experience is always great, but to learn, and then apply, is a much sweeter method.

There is nothing better than a woman who knows what she is talking about. With that said... never stop learning. Continue to educate yourself and learn to be great at everything you do. When I was in high school, I worked at a pizza place in downtown Baltimore. My cousin, Shawn, is a lot like my dad. He may not have made the best choices, but he is filled with wisdom. When I told him that I was a cashier at a pizzeria he said, "That's good. What else have you learned there?" My response was, "I'm not there to learn, I'm there to get paid." He looked over at me and shook his head. He said, "Shanelle, I don't care where you are. Every experience is an opportunity to learn something new. Think out of the box, learn how to make pizza, or talk to the manager about advertising." Back then all I could think was, *"Shawn please just shut up and get me home."* I did not realize that another seed was being planted in me. That was about fifteen years ago, and I still remember that conversation.

You will not learn everything you need to know in school. As a matter of a fact eighty, maybe ninety percent, of what you need to know will be learned through experience and mistakes. The goal is to master them.

I have a tendency of doing different things at one time. It's the creative and entrepreneur in me, but I realized things don't get done that way. I have to master one craft before moving to the next. This is the most difficult life lesson for me, but it works.

I Am Who I Am...Deal with It

Sometimes we allow people to tell us who we are and how we should look. Don't do that! I spent years imprisoned to myself. There were so many things that I wanted to do growing up, and even in my twenties, that I did not do, because I was concerned of how people would see me. For years, I wanted to dye my hair blonde. No good reason; just because I wanted to. But, I never did. I lived in fear over the most ridiculous things. In high school, I didn't do it, because I thought it would break my hair off and I would stand out too much. Well, its just hair; and you only live once. I used to be afraid of what other people would think or how I would be viewed if I walked into an audition. I cared so much that when someone else did something to change his or her look, I would get down on myself because of my insecurities. So, recently, I decided I was going to dye my hair blonde; and I did it! I absolutely love it! I felt a release instantly. I felt beautiful and more confident. The transformation was not really about the blonde hair; any look can change how you feel. But, this was much deeper than that. It was about spiritual fulfillment. I lost a little of who I used to be and I wanted to see the more mature goddess in that girl. I want to test the limits and be courageous enough to do what I want. I want to be spontaneous! If the casting directors can't see past my beautiful, bombshell hair, then that's on them.

Do not live your life by someone else's rules, because you are going to regret it. Girl, you will only live one time. Stop passing up things that bring you joy or make you feel a little more confident. Seriously, it is detrimental to your health! You will wish that you took risks and did things that were more exciting than just talking about what you want to do. Be bold, courageous and of course be creative.

Listen. You Might Learn Something

My husband has told me over and over again that I don't listen. I heard it so much that when he talks, I just shut up so that I can hear exactly what he is saying and the emotion behind it. Although he will still say I'm not listening, I have learned so much from keeping my mouth shut. (I especially learned that when I'm listening, I'm still not listening...If you let him tell it.) You never realize how much you learn from a person when you just listen and observe. People will tell you their whole life and sometimes their motives. Listening helps you to hear the inner monologue of what the person is really saying. You are able to weave out the true essence of the conversation.

People become more interested in you when you show interest in whatever they are talking about. It can also build confidence in a person to know that someone has interest in him or her.

My mother is a talker, and she is hilarious; but one thing that I have noticed is that she rarely takes time to listen to others when she is in a conversation. She has a tendency of cutting people off in the middle of a statement. She does this subconsciously, and sometimes I have to remind her when she is cutting me off. People just want us to shut our trap, open our ears, and give your opinion when you are permitted to. I know it sounds cruel, but it's even more crueler to cut a person off or show no interest when they are trying to communicate with you.

In the heat of a disagreement can be the hardest time to keep your mouth shut. I struggled with this from time to time. So, here is the thing, everyone will feel a lot more appreciated if they can get what they need to say off of their chest and move on. At least, this is what I believe. I could be wrong.

I must confess...I have a problem, as well. Well, I used to have a problem, but I monitor it now. Anyway, I am a rambler. And I have been that way for some years now. Sometimes, I get so excited (Ms. Overdramatic) that I will ramble on in my conversation, to the point that it doesn't even make sense anymore. Or, I will over-explain or give too much information. This is one characteristic about myself that I absolutely hate. If you are a rambler, like me, just take a second before responding and gather all of your thoughts. Do not get so caught up in a conversation that you can't stop talking. Think before you speak and try to make as much sense as possible so that you don't over-explain.

Now, enough embarrassing facts about me!

So, this is where you have some homework to do. Use your personal growth activity page and write down some things that you would like to change about yourself. Whatever will help you to progress in life or make you more confident about yourself. It may be your wardrobe or how you communicate with others. Write down what you want to change, what you will do to change it, and how you will maintain that change. It can be more than one, and if you need more space use your journal.

Personal Development

Things I would like to change about myself are:

To change, I will:

I will maintain the change by:

While living in Baltimore, I took a job as a rehabilitation specialist for troubled young girls. I also taught at an acting and modeling school, which allowed me to, once again, pour knowledge into young souls. They were the most fulfilling jobs that I had ever had. At that time, Chloe'Rae was about two years old, so I already had a little soul to pour into. But, there was something about pouring into a complete stranger that filled me up. Although, I worked for companies that only cared about the money, I would go above and beyond to plant seeds in these young women. It was something that I watched my mother do for young men and women for so many years. I wanted to change lives just as she had done. If there is no one close to you that is pouring positivity into your spirit, I highly suggest that you find someone who will. I am telling you the same things I told those girls, with a few trips and activities added. There is nothing wrong with learning from someone else or confiding in them when you need to.

Confidence comes from creating something and knowing what I'm supposed to be doing, and feeling like I'm good at what I am supposed to be doing.

-Issa Rae

It took me quite a long time to develop a voice, and now that I have it, I am not going to be silent.

-Madeline Albright

LESSON EIGHT

Who Are You, Anyway?

Learning You

Always take time and take inventory of your life and who you are. How do you feel about yourself? Where are you mentally, physically, and emotionally? Are the people in your circle helping you to elevate or are they dragging you down? Are you the smartest person you know? If so, you need to definitely evaluate your circle. Are there habits that you need to change? What path are you on? Take time to ask yourself a few questions. Dump all of your questions and feelings out into a journal. You could do this once a year or once a month, whatever works for you. This will help you to be more aware of who you are and where you want to go. It will also help you to eliminate people and situations out of your life. There is nothing like having positive vibes.

Delete, Delete, Delete!

Post! People! Habits! Relationships! Insecurities! To become the best YOU possible, you have to delete the foolishness that is holding you back from your highest potential. You may feel limited if you are a teenager, but if you have one stitch of poison in your life, it can be detrimental to your health. I spent a lot of time trying to fix the bad instead of letting it go and starting fresh. Don't cheat yourself out of a better life, better choices, or a better you.

Okay…so, I know you're still young and you're just living, but, let me say this...What you put on the internet will be there forever! So, please, pretty young thang, stop putting all of your business and foolish posts up on your social network profiles. If you are going to act a complete fool, don't put it up for the whole world to see. One day, you're going to grow up and you will set a standard about yourself. You may decide that you want to run for mayor or something, but out there in the universe somewhere are videos of you having a twerk session or cursing someone out in a post. Now, if that is what you want to be known for then, by all means, baby girl, do your thing! I found an old Facebook account that I opened in college. I couldn't believe the language I was using or some of the pictures I posted. Surely, I have grown a lot since then. It took me a few hours, but I remembered that password and I deleted the whole account. I was young and didn't know any better, but just seeing it made me cringe.

They say that with consistency, you can start or break a habit in twenty - one days. Now, I'm going to be honest. Breaking habits have never been easy for me. I will try over and over again until I finally get in a rhythm and see some progress. I do know that bad habits are easily started and hard to live with. Good habits are easy to live with, but can be hard to produce. Changing your bad habits will set you up for a better future. Most successful people practice good habits and have rituals to carry out their day. It's a sense of achievement on a daily basis and discipline, which is something you will definitely need. If you research habits of successful people, you will find that most of them do the same thing. Wake up, pray, meditate, or both; eat breakfast, exercise, go over their goals and to-do lists, then focus on whatever their business may be. I'm sure everyone does something different, but whatever the ritual is, the big idea is to make it a habit. I follow the ritual from above, but some days it's out of order, some days some things are missing. The goal is to do your best at bringing good habits in to your life. You will never be perfect.

We've discussed relationships a few times and we will discuss them a little more. That's because relationships can be detrimental to your health and your everyday life. Or, they can be the most positive factors in your life. A past relationship; whether it's love, friendship, or business, can have an effect on how you deal with people in the future. If you have had a past relationship where someone has taken your trust for granted, it will change the way you see people. My advice is to choose your relationships wisely. It's okay to ease your way in, because you may have a hard time stepping away if you need to. If you end up in a bad situation, my next piece of advice is to learn from the situation and how you handled it, then move on.

Insecurities? Delete! Delete! Delete! The only place in the world that you have to live for the rest of your life is in your own skin! So, get comfortable and love it! No one is perfect; and I don't care what you do to your body, you never will be. Everyone has imperfections, even your WCW. Every woman on Instagram, you're following; has at least one thing about themselves that they don't like, but you will never know it. You will never look like her or be her, you will only be you; so, just be the best you. I am not saying this in a negative way. The world that we live in is so vain, and social media makes everything look so easy and glamorous, but what you see is not always what you get. Love yourself and if there is something you don't like, fix it. It's your body and it's your life, just don't get carried away and know that imperfection is beautiful.

Social Media Can Kill You or Make You Stronger

Social media can be a great advantage in your life, or it can have you in counseling. Most young people get influenced by what they see, and that influence becomes a part of their life. You may find yourself inspired by another woman because she is a go-getter, or falling in the comparison trap, which I am sure we have all done at some point or another. If you are one of those girls who compare yourself to other girls let me just say this... STOP! Believe me, it is so dangerous for your self-esteem and how you operate on a day to day. Yes. I know, because I have been that girl, too. Wondering how her life is so great and I am still trying to figure things out. While you are busy scrolling through that girl's page, she is out here doing one of two things...stunting for the 'gram or getting her coins.

A few times a year, I take a break from social media. I log out of my accounts and try to put my focus elsewhere. I learned a few things: that I had an addiction to scrolling, I got so much more accomplished, and I had a clear mind to focus on more than that cute outfit Adrienne (Bailon) Houghton or Marjorie Harvey had on (I love them). Although, they, amongst others, have wardrobes that I would love to sink my teeth into, I cannot scroll through their pages all day. I have things to do and goals to achieve; so, therefore, those "likes" have got to wait! Test yourself and go two days without touching your phone. No social media or texting. Make time for something else; something different. If two days is too much, just do a day or a few hours. I promise you it will make a difference.

Our phones are major distractions in our lives. Now that we are able to record and take pictures of everything, we rarely take time to just live. Nothing is sacred or personal anymore. It separates us from the real world and real time. My wedding was in Ocho Rios, Jamaica, and a few of my close family members were not able to make it so my mom videotaped it and posted it to social media. I cringe every time I think about it, because it was a moment in my life that I wanted to have to myself. Honestly, I felt violated, but I allowed it to happen anyway. I later posted pics, as well, but there was just something about letting everyone into that space that made me very uneasy. We have to learn how to live in the moment and know that every moment is not about impressing everyone. That's what social media is about, isn't it? We post pictures to impress our viewers. If Beyoncé is standing in front of you singing while staring in your eyes, that is not a time to put your phone in her face! Bask in the moment, my dear. Put the phone down and appreciate the moment.

Everyone's Opinion

Your life will be filled with everyone's "say so." People will always have an opinion of who you are, who you should be, what you should be doing, and whom you should be doing it with. One thing that I love about my baby sister is that she does not care about what other people think. There is a hairstylist I admired in my early years that told me that she does not get affected by what people think about her, because the only people that matter are the people who know her best. I totally agree with that statement. I grew up caring so much about what people thought of me that it made me weak and even more insecure. It's like asking someone to be your friend a million times, but they shut you down. No! Their opinion of you and what they think doesn't matter! If it doesn't work for me, I'm not going to entertain it.

Opinions can be about something as small as what college you should go to. When someone gives you an opinion, you can make a choice to hear them out and evaluate what they are saying, or you can just block them out totally. I would only recommend someone being blocked out if they are coming to you from a negative angle. Shadiness has no place here, boo. If the person is giving you a piece of advice, just hear them out, and if you don't agree, that is fine; but, take time to listen. Sometimes people may see something that you don't see.

Don't let others choose your destiny! I know I talk a lot about figuring out what you want to do and strategize; and, yes, I believe you should. However, I know that it can be unrealistic for some of us to be so young and be sure of how you want to spend your life. You may change careers five times before the age of forty; and that is okay! You only get one life and you should be able to explore it however you see fit. Just makes sure you do your research and prepare for whatever. Most importantly, DO NOT LET ANYONE ELSE CHOOSE YOUR DESTINY. Your destiny belongs to you. That is between you and your maker. This is your life, and you have to live with it. One thing that is guaranteed, while you are on this planet, you will always be in your own skin. You can never escape it. So, make choices that you know you can live with. Create the person that you want to become!

Don't let someone else's opinion define you!

Purging Your Mind...

Purge! Yes, I said purge! There are a few movies about purging, but in the sense of the movies, it's about spending one day to be able to legally kill people. That is insane! But, when I say "purge," I mean, to spend time to kill the bad energy and negative thoughts in your mind. We may have covered this, but, oh well, I'm saying it again. And, I might say it again, because it is one of the most important topics in this book and in life. You cannot perform well as a human being if your mind is messed up.

Definition of purging - rid of an unwanted feeling, memory or condition, typically giving a sense of cathartic release.

Purge your mind of all negative thoughts that keep you away from being your highest self.

Your mind can be at two extremes. It can wander all over the place, which can force you to lose focus. Losing focus will cause you to be indecisive and possibly fall off track. They say an idling mind is the devil's workshop. I totally agree, because I have been there. That is the moment that your mind will be attacked with so much negativity. Do not live the life of a person who idles mentally or physically. It says, "This person has no direction or values." Most people who do not know or believe in their self-worth becomes an idler. A lazy person; a person with no vision, no expectations, no voice. They become destructive in their life and maybe someone else.

Take inventory of your thoughts. What I mean is, think about what you're thinking about. What you say and what you think can be the greatest weapons formed against you, or they can be what saves you. With that said, you have to also be selective of what you are hearing. There is a subliminal message in everything around us. Our music, television, magazine ads, even our family and peers. If you hear it or see it, you have the option to let it submerge into your mind. I was watching an interview by an actress who stars on a hit drama series. She said that she doesn't read ratings and critique reviews, good or bad. She has made the decision to not take in any energy that may tamper with her performance. She knows what she can and cannot take. Therefore, she has boundaries set.

As you grow into a woman, there will be a lot of advice given to you. What career path to take, how to be a wife and/or a mother, what dress to wear, where to travel. The list will go on and on. One thing that I've learned from all of this, is that it all does not apply to me. So, I chose to filter what will work for me and what doesn't.

Doubt and disbelief are very relevant in this subject. You have to immediately purge on those thoughts, because they will eat you alive if you let them. One thought can turn into action, and that one action can change your life. I know what negative thoughts can do to you. I am just coming into myself. I consider myself a late bloomer or maybe everyone else has just been playing pretend.

Stress Is A Good Thing!

I often hear my mother say, "I am stressed out!" I've heard it ever since I was a little girl. Then when I got old enough to understand stress I used the phrase too. People see stress as being something that wears you down. It can wear you down, if you only see it as a negative thing. Stress should motivate change. If something is stressing you out or making you frustrated, that means that there needs to be a change there. If you are in a situation that is stressing you out, you will have to get mad enough to want to make things different. Don't whine and cry about it. Complaining only makes things worst. I used to complain about everything, then I realized that the more I complained, the worse I felt, and the worse things got. It's like waking up with a bad attitude. If you do not change your attitude, your whole day will go bad. You will stump your toe getting out the bed, spill juice on your clothes, get a failing grade on your test, or your boyfriend may break up with you… all in one day; but if you don't sweat the small stuff, you allow room for more positivity. Without stress, people would never know how strong they are or what they are capable of. Losing your job can be a good thing if it's going to give you enough time to work on that business you've always wanted, or finish the college applications that you have been putting on the back burner.

Remember my little sister, the pastry chef? She called me one day, upset, because her pay was dropped. All she could think about was her bills. I know this feeling so well. I have been through it a few times. When this kind of stress is laid on you, it could be two things: it's time to move forward or you have gotten too comfortable with your situation. I think that for her, it was both. She had gotten very comfortable with the money she was making; and it was very good money for an eighteen-year-old; even a twenty- eight-year-old. She also has her own cake and dessert company called, "The Pastry Junkie." She spent more time at work than making her cakes, which she sold for profit. My advice to her was to put more energy into building her company than into finding a new job. Stress is the time where most millionaires are born.

> *Follow your own instincts. If you have a dream you have to go after it full throttle, period.*

Now Do Something!

God has His way of placing burning desires in our hearts. It's His way of getting us to our purpose. Even if where you start is not your exact purpose, He may be revealing the stepping stone to your calling. So, please answer it! One thing that I have had issues with during my life is being indecisive. Most people may say, from the outside looking in, that I have it all figured out, but that is not true. The truth is, over the years it has taken me time to make decisions, and sometimes I have been forced to make decisions. Being indecisive has held me back in my past and has filled me with fear to move on ideas and opportunities. The moment I make a decision, I have faith and I jump; and it always comes together. Do not allow your self to sit and ponder on decisions for too long. Get up and do something!

The day after my high school graduation, my mother burst through my bedroom door at eight o'clock in the morning screaming, "Rise and Grind, baby girl!" I wanted to toss her out of the window. She pulled my freshly washed blanket off of my head and forced me out of the bed. I was pissed! She said to me, that in life, there isn't a summer vacation; you work and you get rewarded, but you don't just lay around until noon. School was over, and it was time for me to make some decisions over my life. I was not enrolled in college yet, and at the time, I wasn't working. So, I had to get out and get my own money. We do not get the luxury of just laying around when you have no accomplishments, no money, and no vision. Celebrate your achievements and move on. The moment that you feel you have done all that you can do and you have no more goals or obstacles to overcome, and there is simply nothing left, then you can stop moving and spend the rest of your life relaxing; but even then, you will find something else that may tickle your fancy. Don't lay in your bed all day wishing and hoping and dreaming...get up and do something!

Dream Big, Wake Up, and Work for It!

Big Brother Diddy! (No, he is not my real brother, but you and I have already had that conversation.) Diddy has been the best motivator that a girl can ask for! From his music, to his speeches, to his Instagram posts, to his every day attitude. I absolutely love it! His mantras, "Can't Stop, Won't Stop," and "Lock In" have kept me going and kept me focused during those days when I felt like I was falling apart. He has an energy and confidence that we all should possess. One thing that resonated with me was his speech at Howard University. After finding out he was having a baby, and losing his job working for a well-known record company, his first thought was, *"What am I going to do now?"* One day, you will be stuck in between a rock and a hard place, and you will have to make decisions to push you forward. This will be the first question you will ask yourself..."What am I going to do now?" This is your turning point. You don't have time to idle, you don't have time to complain, and you don't have time to sleep through it. This is your chance to DREAM BIG! Then wake up and get to work!

> *Your time is precious my love...*

You cannot dream big and envision a life of big cars and a nice house, but you dedicate most of your time to just dreaming, complaining, or everything else. You have to spend more than four hours a week on your dream. I heard this on a Youtube video years ago and I remember thinking, *"Wow! This is me!"* I spent more time complaining, wishing, and hoping, than actually going after what I wanted. If I would have stayed the course, no telling what heights I would have reached by now. Again, not a regret, but a lesson learned. As I said before, distractions are a trap to keep you away from your purpose. And anything can be a distraction if you let it.

You may be studying for a final or creating a new line of fashion and get a phone call from your mom who just called to say hello, but the conversation leads to what happened at work. This will not only change your focus, but it may affect your energy. Especially if it is a conversation filled with drama. For example, before my mother moved to Atlanta with us, she would call me in the morning around seven thirty. By then, I would have dropped my oldest daughter off to school and I would be preparing to go work out. I had to give her boundaries as well as, everyone else who called me. "Ma, no ratchet-ness before 9AM." This means no drama! No gossiping! Nothing that would poison my vibrations or my thoughts. I needed to stay focused, workout, and complete all of my tasks first. I have a girlfriend who I have set boundaries with as well. I love her and her energy for the most part, but I also know that we will indulge in gossip at some point during our conversation. In order to protect my peace and my focus, I have to set boundaries.

We have all fallen into the trap of scrolling until your fingers hurt, and before you know it, an hour has gone by and you have looked at everyone's feed. You are so caught up in their accomplishments that you forget about your own to-do list. By the time you are done scrolling, you are so exhausted and feeling less confident than you did before, because you have filled your mind with a bunch of fluff that cannot possibly help you to complete your goals. Let's stop watching everyone else live his or her dreams and invest in our own. What do you say?

Anyone that is successful will tell you that they had to sacrifice something in their life, and hard work was key. Beyoncé sacrificed her childhood; she spent the majority of her childhood preparing to be the star that she is today. These days, I'm sure she sacrifices sore feet, because there is no other who can dance in a pair of heels like Bey. It doesn't stop with Beyoncé. The list goes on and on. Everything around you was sacrificed before being produced. That outfit that you have on…the vision had to start somewhere; and time, energy, money, and I'm sure other things that we don't know about. There will be days that you have to focus and lock in. You won't be able to go to the movies and hang out with your friends. You have to focus until the job is done. This is a trait that you want to hold on to.

PCP

All of this rolls up into three terms…Procrastination, Consistency and Persistence. Please understand, these are definitely parts of my life I have not mastered along with discipline (lol), but I'm working on it; seriously I am. But, just because I have not mastered them does not mean I should share the knowledge. Girl! Okay, for starters, I can't really call myself a procrastinator, but I will say I have the tendency from time to time. Procrastination is the thief of time and energy. There are a few reasons why we procrastinate: laziness, lack of confidence, fear of failing, or you may just feel like the goal you are trying to achieve is boring. It's a lot easier to look busy when really, you are procrastinating. The more you procrastinate, the further you are away from the achievement.

Consistency is to discipline yourself in a manner that you will commit yourself to something. This is where I am putting my focus. I would say that commitment makes me nervous, but that is a lie, because I'm married. However, I do have issues with committing to daily activity. Social media, is a great example. It took me a long time to not only find interest in *Instagram*, but to look at social media as a business tool and not just a hobby. With that said, the inconsistency showed in my feeds. I didn't post regularly, and my post rarely served my image. This type of behavior also showed up in other parts of my life, which I talk about throughout the book. Not just you, but *we* have to work harder at committing ourselves and being consistent. Without making this a habit, you will be unfocused and indecisive; which will soon lead to you delaying your opportunities.

What major event, situation or goal in your life should you be focused on right now?

____

____

What is your biggest distraction that delays you from achieving it?

____

____

List a few ways that you can stop yourself from being distracted. Hold yourself accountable to stay away from them.

____

____

Is there a dream that you possess? If so, what is it?

____

____

Make a plan to keep you from procrastinating. Find something you want to do and commit to it!

Is there someone that you admire who carries your same dream? If so, do your research and find out what they had to sacrifice to make their dreams come true. Do not allow the outcome to scare you away. It should only make you aware of the work you need to put in to make your dreams come true.

One day the people who didn't believe in you will tell everyone they meet how they know you.
-ThinkPynk

There are two conflicting philosophies that I love. Everyone thing happens for a reason; as well as, you can change everything that you have control over.
-Yara Shahidi

I thrive on obstacles. If I've been told that it can't be told, then I push harder.
Issa Rae

LESSON NINE

It's Not Depression, It's Life!

Mama Said it Would Be Days Like This

Life can throw us for a loop. You will end up in situations that you never saw coming. Especially when you think that you have it all figured out. It can get rough, but you cannot get so caught up in how bad it is that you can't get passed it. When we are feeling down about ourselves, we have a tendency of bringing more bad energy to us. We complain and feel bad about ourselves. The whole nine! Do not wallow in self-pity. Go ahead and cry it out. Confide in a friend if you need to. Then, get up, wipe your tears, and keep it moving! Things may never be exactly how you want them to be. You may fall to the very bottom, but the great thing is, you are still here, you are healthy, and able to make a change in your life! Do not pass up on that opportunity! Take it! The longer you sit and think about how you are failing in life and how everything is going wrong the worse it will get. Purge! Be proactive; talk yourself into a good mood. "I look good! I feel good; and it's all good!" Yeah, it's a little corny, but my daughter says it, so I love it!

At the beginning of the book, I talked about my first experience with living on my own. I put college on hold and I got a full-time job as a debt collector. This story is one of the biggest lessons of my young adult life. Not just, because of the builds. I also went through something spiritually and mentally.

Yes, I loved the independence, but I could have done a few things different. Like I would have saved more money so that I could enjoy life while I was working to pay my bills, and I would have put together an exit plan; but you live and you learn. After a while, I quit the job and moved on to a very similar job that I hated even more.

Finally, I took the test for my cosmetology license. Was it easy? Heck no! I passed the practical on my first try, but I took the written test at least four times and, finally, I passed. I'm back on top! I'm about to step in an industry that I love and studied through high school, I have a nice furnished home, a nice car, my Neiko, and a little something in the bank to hold me over for a while. I found a job in a salon working on commission, and I was happy. Then, life happens. My father was sick in the hospital. My father and I were beginning to rebuild our relationship. During my teenage years, we could barely stand to be in the same room as each other. We both made mistakes. He spent a lot of time incarcerated, and I was angry that he left me for so long, but I wanted to start off fresh. He couldn't bear to accept that I was no longer a little girl anymore, and tried to control my every move; so, naturally we bumped heads. After I moved out on my own, our relationship started to shift into a better space.

At the age of twenty, I faced what I thought was just a hospital visit, but it turned out to be my daddy's last days. June 22, 2007 at 12:23am was the day I watched my dad take his last breath. It was the most soul crushing feeling that I had ever felt in my entire life. At that time, nothing could make me feel worse than that.

That was one time in my life that I felt regret for all of the things I've said in the past and not spending a lot of time trying to make things better. After that day, I spent three or more years depressed. I moved from salon to salon and I was not making any money. I lost my house and my car two years after losing my dad. Anthony and I were in a really bad place in our relationship and we finally broke it off. I was just a mess! A complete mess! What's funny, is that no one really knew. I didn't go to counseling or anything, I just allowed myself to go through it. Which I can honestly say was not the best idea. I felt completely alone. My mother was going through her own grieving and I didn't feel like I had a friend in the world. As a matter of a fact, one of my closest friends from high school turned her back on me.

Life became too much to handle, and at one point I really thought about slipping away just so I couldn't feel the pain anymore. But, I knew that I had a deeper purpose in my life. I just had to take time to discover it. I had to find myself, again, and rebuild her. It took a lot of work for me to get to this point, and I am still working on myself 'til this day.(I feel like this is a moment to say; if you have ever thought about harming yourself in any way because of some things you have been through; please understand that every day you wake up is a new day and a new chance to redeem yourself and serve your purpose. As long as you can wake up, you can get up and make a change.) I could not allow all of the things that I was going through to keep me away from my purpose.

Like I said, life is going to take you for a loop. You will have situations that feel like they are way too hard to handle, but just know that there is always a solution. You have to calm yourself and evaluate the situation, and then attack! Depression who? Not you!

I have a cousin who confides in me often. However, she called me crying and saying that she can't deal with life anymore, she's losing it, and she is depressed. All she does is cry. She is not happy with who she is or how she looks. I had no idea this is what she was going through, because from the outside looking in, she was living and she owns her look. She is a beautiful woman; she travels often and has a good career going. She struggles with her weight, but she is absolutely gorgeous with a heart that can overshadow this planet. She felt like people have treated her wrong, and she has no idea what she should be doing with her life. She was on a career path that was pretty much pushed on her. For years, I told her she should be in fashion or beauty, because those were the parts of her that she did effortlessly. At this time, she was in her mid-twenties. Those twenties are something else! Around the mid-twenties, we start evaluating ourselves and where we are in our lives. You may feel great and hopeful, or you may feel scared and stuck, but just know it is only for a season. She found herself needing professional help. Yes, sometimes we may need to hear a professional's opinion. But, take it from me…medication and a doctor diagnosing you with personality disorders is not always what's best. You do not need an excuse to feel worse about yourself or lazy. You need someone to say, "Girl, take a few days in a quiet place, relax your mind, journal a little, pray, and get your mind right! God has something out there for you and your job is to get out there and get it!" I am proud to say that, yes, she struggles from time to time, but she got back up and got on her grind.

Depression will last for as long as you let it! I know, because I have had my fair share; but, the moment you make the decision to feel better and do better, life will turn around. Whenever you have a bad thought of things going wrong, take a deep breath and think about all of those great things that you love about yourself and the plans you are focusing on. If you come to a crossroad and you don't know who you are or what you want to become, sit down again and re-valuate yourself. *"Who am I? What do I want? Where am I going? How will I get there?"* If you feel bad about yourself immediately, find a way to change that. You are the only person responsible for your life and how it pans out. No one else can make your life great but you; so get on the job!

Independence Just Ain't Fun Anymore

As women, we all want a sense of independence. You want to own something and feel great about it. That's fine, but just know that it is not always fun and games. It's kind of like getting a visible tattoo or marriage; you have to commit to it. You can't move out today and get a job, then, decide you don't want it anymore. Even if you gave it all up, your independence will carry over to something else. If you want to travel the world, you will still have to find a way to eat and live without sleeping on the sidewalk. If you know that you are in a good situation, but, it is not where you want to stay, just make sure you have a plan - an exit plan to your next destination. Don't spend all of your money or rent a place that's going to take your whole paycheck, because then, you will not have enough to fall back on when you make changes in your life. Try not to bite off more than you can chew. Gain some experience in this thing called independence, and then, make spontaneous decisions. Now, don't get me wrong, I am one to believe in faith, but faith and a plan will keep you from a lot of detours in life. Independence also means financial freedom. Yes, of course, we will take a few bucks from our parents when it is offered, but if you are going to be independent, don't spend your whole life looking for your parents to pull you out of every situation. As an adult, you have a responsibility to take care of yourself. Call your parents when you have exhausted all avenues. If they give you a large amount of money from a trust fund or birthday, don't just blow it on shoes and clothes;

make wise decisions that will set you up for a better life or experience.

No More Victim

After my father's death, I spent numerous amounts of time mad with him. I was mad that he left me here to figure out life alone. I was mad that he left my mother alone. I was mad about our disagreements from the past. I was mad that he didn't take time to know me for me. I was mad that he took so much of my father and daughter moments away and locked them up in a cage with him. I was mad! What made it worse was that I would never get it back. He told me he loved me and he lectured me with good advice, but we were both too prideful to look each other in the eyes and say, 'I'm sorry.' Because of that, I was bruised and my heart was beaten. I wallowed in this pity for years, which was eighty percent of where my depression festered. I saw a counselor who talked about nothing but her self, so that didn't help. I couldn't talk to my mother, because at the time, her only focus was her own pain, so I had to live in it. Then, I realized that there is nothing I can do about the past. Nothing! All I can do is forgive myself and forgive my dad so that I can move on. No, it was not easy, and I still deal with his death every day. But, the moment that I let go of the bad stuff and focused on the good, blessings were revealed. You cannot stay a victim forever. It's like an infected organ. If it is not removed, it will infect all of the other organs and your body will eventually shut down.

Let Go!

Your past does not define you. As I've said a million times, we all make mistakes. What matters is how you get up from them. We all come from a different walk of life. Your walk will be totally different from mine, and so will the mistakes. I have connected with homeless people, teen moms, people who have spent time in jail, trouble makers, drop outs - the list goes on. Some of my mentors have been in these situations, plus some. They went through what they went through and then they moved on. Just because a person is homeless, doesn't mean they will be there forever. There may be a teen mom reading this right now, so I am speaking to you. Yes, you may be going through life with a baby on your hip, but this cannot stop you or define you. You still have a chance at making a great life for you and your child. There are teen moms in this world who are millionaires. I am not saying that you made a good choice, but I am saying that you should work harder than you did before to build yourself a great future. Instead of saying, "I can't be successful, because I have this kid," say, "I will be successful, because I have this kid." DO NOT GIVE UP!

Okay, so now that I have spilled that out…

So, you've failed a class or two, or you embarrassed yourself in the worst way possible. So, what?! Yes, I said it…So, what!? It's not that I am not sensitive to your situation. I just know that life is not about falling on your face and laying your head on the concrete. It's about rebuilding, growing, and getting to your purpose. You cannot do that if you are standing in the spilled milk from two years ago. It's spoiled and it smells horrible! Get up off the concrete and clean up the spilled milk!

If You Don't Like It, Leave

If your situation makes you mad, but you are still in it, then, you are insane. How judgmental of me, right? Maybe I am being judgmental, but I've also been there. In friendships, jobs, houses, career paths, even my relationship. Sometimes it takes a person to get angry to make a well-needed change in their life. Let me tell you how backwards I used to be. I had no patience for things that made me happy, but I had more patience with the things that made me unhappy. It sounds crazy, but a lot of people do it. Choosing to sit in the house, bored to death, instead of choosing to spend time with friends or going to the movies. If something is happening in your life that you know is bringing you a bad feeling, DELETE IT!

It is important to give things a chance, but do not become naive. If you are in a relationship with a guy and he does not make you feel an ounce of joy, then you should move on. That's the same with friendships, jobs, etc. If your job makes you miserable, then put together an exit plan. That means, find a job that will make you happy, or start your own business. And, yes, you can start your own business in high school; stop limiting your ability. It may not be as easy to delete a teacher that you don't like, so in this situation do your best to get through it, because next year, you will have to deal with a new teacher that you may like. So, just brace yourself.

I recently had to let go of a friendship that I had for years. That person had no value in my life and was filled with negativity. As much as I love her, I had to make a decision. I didn't call her and say, "We cannot be friends anymore." I just decided to love her from a distance. People, places, and things can be toxic in your life, and there is no reason to keep them around. You cannot change who, what, or where they are, so, your best bet is to put on your big girl panties and move on. This also means family. A lot of the times we give family a pass. I am a very family-oriented person. I have always tried to do good by my family, but there have been times when I have felt outcast and unappreciated, even disrespected. Instead of loving those people from a distance, I would let things die, then, come back around to get shot in the foot, again. I am not saying to not forgive. I am saying; protect your peace. Sometimes you have to drop off family just like everyone else. Sometimes you have to allow time to mend things and sometimes you just need to stay away. Toxic is toxic, period!

When Is It My Time to Shine?

I have spent numerous amounts of hours studying big brother Tyler Perry's business ethic and watching his speeches online, along with a few other mentors of mine. On his website, he used to have, what he called, "The Motivational Corner." This is where he expressed his life lessons and sent an inspiring message to those who needed it. One thing that resonated with me is when he said, "Sometimes, God has you hidden." As the message continued, he talked about how God had him hidden for years before his work was introduced to the world. You have to prepare for your moment to shine. The goal is lifelong success; not a quick social media come up that may not last very long. Put time and work into whatever it is that you are focused on. Quality is much more important than quantity. In due season, your hard work will be available for the world to see. On the flip side to that, please do not sit around saying, "When will it be my time?" but you have done nothing to make that time come. There needs to be some kind of action behind that, even if it's a little at a time.

As a creative and an Aries woman; I can be impatient. I have gone through the whole "When is it my time, God?" speech a thousand times over. I may have even been a brat about it. The lessons that I have learned are: This will not be the last time that I have this "When is it my time?" moment, and God works on His own time, not mine. And, the more I sit around going through this, the more time and energy I am wasting. For these reasons I am blessed to have people around me to say, "Shanelle, you're trippin,' again. Get yourself together and G up." (In case you have no street education, "G up" means take it like a man and do what you gotta do. Be a gangsta.) These type of moments do not feel good. It makes your whole day dark and depressing. You will become resentful and envious to those around you who are living their best life. It's a mental trap that you don't want to get stuck in.

There have been many of days when I wondered when my time would come. I would fall into a deep depression, because I felt like I was working so hard and I wasn't being noticed. The older I got, the more I noticed that I spent a lot of time being busy, but not as productive. I was anxious and wanted something so bad, but I never sat back to realize that I wasn't working as hard or as smart as I needed to. These habits, alone, were the reason I was not where I wanted to be. I would go to events, meet people, and do a little networking, but I would never follow up with them later. I put every distraction possible before my craft and my focus. I tried to skip steps to get to my destination, and sometimes I took too many steps to get to my destination. But, one of the worst habits I had was not investing more into myself - whatever that meant at the time. If I would have put most of my energy into my craft, I would have come across more opportunities, and I would have been better prepared. Do not cheat yourself and then look for someone to recognize you.

I Love Me, But Not Today

Girl! There is a day or two in every girl's life where she doesn't feel like herself. None of us are perfect; even if her Instagram page says something different. Sometimes you may feel fat, ugly, or not so smart. We are women, so the list goes on and on! This is not uncommon. We all go through it, but that doesn't mean that it is true, and if it is true, then do something about it. If you feel "un-cute" then put on your cutest outfit, your hottest shoe, fix that mop on your head, and rip the runway. If you feel fat, start your day with a healthy meal, take a walk, or run, or maybe take a class at your nearest YMCA or gym. If you feel unintelligent, research something that may excite you, go to your nearest bookstore and indulge into something interesting. These are some of the things that I do when I am feeling any of these emotions. In all honesty, they work. You are fire!

All of these emotions piggyback off of something else that's going on with you. Maybe you have gained weight, but what was the cause of it? Yes, I know food; but what made you eat and gain weight? For example, I work out regularly, but I have had a tendency of falling off sometimes and gaining a few pounds. Usually, it's because something else in my life has fallen out of place. A lot of the time, while working in a salon, I would eat for convenience. There was nothing close to me, but fried chicken and fries or fast food, which I often shy away from. On top of that, I did not prepare my lunch for work the day before.

This happened because I didn't prepare my week effectively by ironing clothes and cooking dinner a few days in advance for my family. So, I would be busy day by day, preparing for the next day, cleaning up, feeding my girls, doing homework, bathing them and spending quality time with my husband, and so on. By the time night fell, I am too tired to work out or get anything else prepared. This forced me to eat what's available during my work day, and snack on sweets. It's a slippery slope.

If your life is a mess, then the way you feel about yourself will most likely be a mess, too. If you feel unhealthy, you may not feel pretty, either. If your room is dirty, you may not be inspired to focus on anything else. (Seriously though, when my house or workspace is clean and smells good I am more inspired to do something.) Getting your life in some kind of order will be the boost you need. Change your day to day habits or whatever is the core to your emotions, and it may all come together for you.

If you have not hit twenty yet, then you are in for a real eye opener. When you turn sixteen, it's exciting, because you are two years from the "I'm Grown" age - eighteen.

Eighteen is where we believe all of our independence lies. This is the year where no one can tell you anything, because you know it all. The sky is the limit and we feel unstoppable. Around the age of twenty, and twenty-one, there are some good and some bad. Yes, you are at the legal age in the United States to go to a bar, but this is when you have to really face reality. It's time to make grown up decisions; and this part is where the work really comes in.

This does not stop at twenty-one. A lot of people go through this phase until the age of twenty-five, when you start realizing that you are five years away from thirty. Yeah, it's a lot of numbers, but this is real. Decision-making can be a challenge, and until you make decisions to move you forward, you will be running in circles.

"If you can believe in something great, I feel you can achieve something great!"

-Katy Perry

"I am a woman, phenomenally. Phenomenal woman, that's me."

-Maya Angelou

"We can't become who we need to by remaining who we are."

-Oprah

LESSON TEN

The Power of A Woman

Women are the most powerful beings on this planet. The problem is, that most of us don't know it. Yes, God made man the head of the household, but the woman is the neck. Without the neck, the man would not have control. Think about it like this if there were no women on this planet, men would walk around in pajamas all day and do nothing at all. Even though they may act like we are incapable of so many things, the truth is most of the ideas they have we have instilled in them some kind of way. Mother, sister, wife, grandmother, girlfriend; we have influence over a large percentage of the decisions they make. However, this is not about men. This is about us.

We are the most caring, nurturing, multi-taskers on this planet. Women are the real hustlers. Sacrificing is something that we do by nature. We will give everything that we have.

There are a few lessons that you need to learn:

1. Self-Accountability- Being a woman means to be responsible and hold yourself accountable. If you make promises, do your best to keep them. Everybody else is not always the problem; sometimes it's you.

2. Own Your Own - There is nothing wrong with having a partner that will split the bills with you, whether it's a boyfriend, husband, sister, or best friend; but, hold your own. Do your part and always be able to take care of yourself if things don't turn out the way you planned. Always have a goal in mind for your life and aspire to own something and have assets to help build a comfortable lifestyle for yourself. That moves on to my next point.

3. Stack Your Money- Always put some money aside. I don't call it a rainy day fund, I call it an opportunities account. Learn how to manage your money. You should not spend your life working to pay bills. If you learn how to manage your money at an early age, you will be a pro by the time you move out on your own. Grab a few money management books from the library or online. As a matter of a fact, Google it.

4. Rise and Grind - Get out here and get what you want with tenacity. Success is the best revenge. If you want to do something, do it! Get started! Life is about trying, failing, and succeeding. Nothing beats a failure but a try. Besides, how else will you learn?

5. Extend Your Hand - There is nothing charming about a selfish person. Your knowledge and your rewards are not just for you. Help someone else.

6. A Cute Face Is Not Everything - I'm going to say it again. There better be some brains behind that cute face, because you will not get far without it.

7. Dreams Matter - Do not give up your dreams to please someone else. Often, as women, we put our needs and wants on hold to please and help everyone else. God gave us visions and dreams for a reason, and they are certainly not meant to be buried in the back of your conscience.

8. Take Back What You Put Out- If you are woman enough to judge, be woman enough to be judged. Criticism can be a hard pill to swallow and no one is exempt from it.

9. Vengeance Is Mine- Like Beyoncé says, the best revenge is your paper. Nothing says, "I won," like success and joy. Hit your haters where it really hurts.

10. L. I. G. - Let It Go! If it's not working for you, move on! Life is too short to be wrapped up in things that are not beneficial to your life. Do yourself a solid and run to the nearest exit.

These are just a few- the list goes on. You will encounter more lessons as you grow and experience life. Be aware of the lessons and learn from them.

There are people in this world that will make you feel like you are less than who you are. They will belittle you, betray you, take advantage of you, and speak ill over your name. That does not give you permission to be who they want you to be. When I think about all of the powerful women in this world and how they have pushed passed the nonsense and trash talking, it makes me feel more powerful, because I know there is a great history of women that have been through far more. They were able to get through being talked about, discriminated against, abuse, and so much more. They found their power and took ownership of it. I don't want to give you a history lesson, but I'm just saying!

I remember I had a close family member tell me to my face that I would never be anything. I had another close family member ask me what kind of mother I was to leave my child to go out to Los Angeles. FYI, I was going to LA for one month to get a home and job established before moving my daughter so far. She would have been cared for by her dad and my mom. These were two women that I love dearly. Both of those family members hurt me with their words, but as the years have went on, I have continued to progress. With that said, people that have no vision of their own will do whatever they can to shut you down. Your job is to not let that happen. As you progress, you will notice that those same people are exactly where you left them. Get your paper! End of story.

> *Be the best* **you** *that you can be unapologetically!*

Own Your Own

It's nothing like having something and saying, "It's mine! I worked hard for it!" When you own your own, it is less likely that someone will take it from you. There are a few titles that millennial women use a lot. "Boss Babe" and "Girl Boss" are my two favorites. It means, to be independent and in charge. It's a title that exudes status, value, and confidence. If you are a "Boss Babe" or a "Girl Boss," you are taking this world by storm; setting goals and achieving them with style.

These titles are earned, even though they are used so lightly. They mean that you are handling your business without people seeing you sweat.

As I said before, I have always found a way to make money. I've been an entrepreneur since a very young age. One thing that I learned with working a regular job was that they were not going to make me rich. Yes, you can retire after a few years, but there will always be a limitation on what you can do, how much you will make, and how you can make it. Of course, you should get a job and experience. Of course, you should choose a career. Of course, you should save for the day that you don't want to work really hard. My advice is to always have a side hustle, or like I said before, an exit strategy. In school, we are taught to get a job or a trade, and that's fine, but they don't tell you that there is a possibility that you can be fired or something can go wrong. So, with that said, baby girl, always have your own, just in case. Equity will hold a lot of value in your future. I know this may not be the most entertaining subject, but if you want to be able to live your life, shop, get a nice car, and do what you want, you better make sure you get on your "Girl Boss" ish.

Be the Person You Need

Be the person that you want everyone else to be for you. Sometimes we look for people to love and support us, but we don't do the same in return. This is not okay. Yes, it is true that sometimes you have to be selfish with our space, energy, and time. But, this should not be a constant excuse for not being there for those who are there for you. Selfish ambitions will cause us to put so much focus into ourselves that we never take a second to see if a friend needs our help or if a family member is doing okay. Take time to show love to someone else. Something as small as a compliment can change the way someone's day is going. Just a simple, "I love your hair," can boost a person's self-esteem. You may be the first person in a long time to give them a compliment. And guess what? It cost you nothing.

Mirror, Mirror on the Wall, Who's to Blame for It All

Woman up! I've mentioned that holding yourself accountable is a part of womanhood. Do we all do it? No, of course not. We have all pointed the finger at someone else for decisions we have made. It may feel good to make someone else your excuse for being messy, but reality is YOU'RE STILL MESSY. Take full responsibility for your actions or you will never change. When you blame everyone else, it gives you permission to continue doing what you're doing. How can you evolve, if it's always someone else fault? I love the song, "Man in the Mirror" by Michael Jackson. He sings, "I'm starting with the man in the mirror. I'm asking him to change his ways. No message could have been any clearer. If you wanna make the world a better place, take a look at yourself and make a change." (Yes, I am singing the song as I type; and yes, the lyrics may be a little off, but you get it.)

You Cute or Whateva

If a cute face and fancy clothes are all that you possess; we have a problem. Most girls who use their looks to get ahead usually don't make it far. At some point, you will have to open your mouth. If you don't sound as beautiful or intelligent as you look, it will either turn people off or have the wrong people running after you. I have a guy friend who was in love with a girl for a long time, but he had never actually met her. He would see her out on the town at different events, but he would never approach her. From across the room, she looks like she is his perfect match. Finally, he asked her out. They went on their first date and immediately he realized she was loud in quiet places, and was very bossy and demanding. To add insult to injury, she couldn't hold a decent conversation past what was the best club in the city. He was completely turned off by her. He said to me, "She was beautiful until she opened her mouth." Now, for some of us that may be insulting, but reality is, you need to know how to turn it on and off. There is a time to be classy and there is a time to be ratchet and have loud outbursts with your friends. I am not saying that you should be someone that you are not. I'm just saying that there is a time and place for everything; and ACT LIKE YOU HAVE SOME SENSE! (In my mother's voice.)

Vengeance is Mine

OMG! How long are you going to be mad? This is my question to myself! Sometimes, I get so caught up in my feelings that I will start finding everything wrong with the person I'm mad at. Wasting all of my energy being mad at them, when I should be out here getting this money! He or she surely is not losing sleep or money over me being mad. Look, check this out...GET OUT OF YOUR

FEELINGS. You are wasting your time and energy. You can't be prosperous and mad at the same time. Move on.

> *Don't lose yourself in negative situations, honey. It's not worth it.*

Disney Binge Watch

I know you are like, "Shanelle, what in the world are you talking about?" Listen, young grasshopper; almost every Disney movie ever made is filled with philosophical gems that will teach you a thing or two about life. I love Disney movies and I made my children fall in love with them, too. You probably think that I am trippin,' but hear me out! Check out a few of these quotes that I have listed from a few of my favorite Disney movies. I'm sure you will find them to be helpful:

"The past can hurt, but you can either run from it, or learn from it."

– Rafiki, *"The Lion King"*

"Laughter is timeless, imagination has no age, and dreams are forever."

– Walt Disney

"Venture outside of your comfort zone, the rewards are worth it."

– Rapunzel, *"Tangled"*

"A little consideration, and a little thought for others will make all of the difference."

– Eeyore, *"Winnie The Pooh"*

"Even miracles take a little time."

-The Fairy Godmother, *"Cinderella"*

"If you focus on what you left behind, you will never be able to see what lies ahead."

-Gusteau, *"Ratatouile"*

"Don't just fly, soar."

-Dumbo

"The problem is not the problem. The problem is your attitude about the problem."

-Jack Sparrow, *"Pirates of the Caribbean"*

I can go on forever. Disney movies are like little life coaches. Maybe this is where my daughter gets her skills. I seriously doubt that you will ever read another self-enhancement book that tells you to watch Disney movies. So what? I will be the first!

Sorry... not sorry...

Don't Be Shady

I'm going to make this one quick and easy. If you are the shady friend or coworker or family member...Stop! It is doing you no justice to be nasty to people. There is nothing to be earned from throwing shade, spreading gossip or starting drama. If you don't like people and would rather be alone, then I am sorry to hear that, because the world is a beautiful place with a lot of beautiful people in it. But, you will never know if you are so busy walking around with a stink face and bad attitude. Ugh! I just don't get it. Please don't take this as judgmental, because it is not. We all go through things and of course you can have your days when you want to be alone or you can't find a smile, but don't make it a permanent thing. You are missing out on how amazing your days could be.

The last salon I worked in really made me look at myself. The owner and I were not the best of friends and my time there was way over do. My energy had changed tremendously. Our feelings towards one another transpired into the energy of the salon. Every time someone said something to me that sound like an inch of shade I was ready for the clap back. Some days I went to work ready for war. I knew then that it was my bitter end. I also realized that I had allowed all of my negative thoughts and feelings to over take me outside of work. It became the conversation of the evening. I know that my husband, my mom and my friends were so tired of hearing about it. The moment I left I felt a burden lifted off of my shoulders. However, I had to check myself before then, because the shade that I would pass back was a waste of my positive energy. I could have been meditating on my next move. Bottom line, unless you are a straight up heartless individual; what you say and how you treat others can also affect you.

What is your definition of womanhood?

____

____

____

____

____

____

"Beauty is when you can appreciate yourself. When you love yourself, that's when you're most beautiful."

-Zoe Kravitz

"All you need is faith, trust, and a little pixie dust."

-Tinker Bell

"Who says that my dreams have to just stay my dreams?"

-Ariel, "The Little Mermaid"

LESSON ELEVEN

Never Despise Small Beginnings

"Never despise small beginnings" is another lesson I learned from Big Brother Tyler. When I heard this, I was like, *"I do not have time to be thinking small!"* Well, it just so happens, he is right! Earlier, I said that you should always learn, even if what you are learning does not align with what you are doing.

It's the same with small beginnings. You may have an idea that is bigger than the universe, such as opening a clothing store. I have a friend from high school who used to wear his own designs to school every day. He would use a color paint and glitter to write the name to his design on his clothes. A few years later, he got shirts printed and was selling the clothes to all of our friends. Soon enough, it got really popular and he was able to make different designs. Now, he has his own boutique, selling his own brand name, and this happened in less than ten years. What makes this so much more amazing is that he worked for all of it. He didn't cheat anybody or steal. He was a boy from the inner city of Baltimore who had a vision, and he attacked it with a vision. That is what's up. The moral of the story is that starting small can grow into something bigger than you ever imagined.

> *Create something for yourself and be relentless!*

For Every Action, There's a Reaction

This should be short and sweet. For every action, there is a reaction. So, there are two lessons that come out of this. The first one is, if you are expecting for something to happen, you have to act on it in order to see some kind of result. Don't be the person that only reacts to things; take action first. Don't wait until a test comes up and then study, or for a bill to be past due to pay on it. That's a reaction. You should have already studied your notes well before testing, even if it is a little at a time. At least you would be further along. There should already be money set aside for the bill you knew was coming. (Now, sometimes things happen. Believe me, I know.) The point that I am making is, stay ready so that you don't have to get ready.

Every opportunity is a Chance for Growth

This statement is very similar to, "Never despise small beginnings." Just because you are in a low position does not mean that is where you will stay. If you are a cashier at McDonald's, don't knock it. Just dream bigger, maybe you dream of opening your own restaurant one day, or owning a McDonald's franchise. Working as a cashier is a great opportunity to learn about customer service and how the restaurant is operated. From there, you can move up in the company until you are in a position to buy your own franchise. This is just an example, but it happens every day. Do not limit your dreams or where an opportunity can take you just because it doesn't start at the top. Be patient with yourself and the process you will need to go through.

Sometimes You Have to Take A Step Back

I used to hate this saying, but it is very true. Sometimes you have to take a step back to take a giant leap forward. There will definitely be a time in your life where you will think everything is falling into place perfectly, and, then, one thing goes wrong that forces you to stop whatever you are doing. Have you ever seen a movie where everything was going great in the characters' lives, but, then, something really bad happens? That situation usually forces them to become their best self and it reveals their strength, which puts them into a better position than what was expected. These situations happen in real life. Allow them to bring you wisdom and growth.

Trust No One

I've heard this statement a few times in my life, but I will be the first to say I have had a few naive moments with trusting people who didn't mean me any good. Of course there will be people in your life that you can genuinely trust everyone is not out to get you. I have had a tendency of sharing my thoughts and genius ideas, as well as, my business. I've learned the hard way that people could care less about your gain, but more about theirs, and they will do all they can to destroy you. Recently, I put together a brief proposal of the book that you are reading. I sent it out to women who I was interested in interviewing for the book. One in particular was an old friend who had made a name for herself as a makeup artist. Before I sent it, something in my gut was telling me not to. A few days later, I saw a post of her speaking to a group of young women with subjects similar to my proposal. For me, it was obvious that she was "inspired" by my work; but, to others, it looked like she was a saint with such a brilliant idea. Yeah, right... I was completely enraged and so upset! I was more upset that she took the opportunity to present what was now a "new passion" of hers from my piece of work. What I feel is not only my passion, but a part of my walk, had been highjacked by an opportunist. I could have been overreacting...maybe, maybe not. The point is, I let her in to something that was close to my heart, something that should have stayed under wraps until it was time to reveal. Don't get so excited about something that you feel everyone is supposed to know about it. Like I said before, there are a lot of snakes in the grass; you have to watch everything and everybody. Believe me when I say, a lot of relationships and a lot of people are not who or what they seem.

I heard a saying that you have to be a sheep in a world full of wolves, with the spirit of a dove. I can't say I fully agree with that. I understand it, but I don't fully agree. I believe that you should have the spirit of a sheep, which is to be gentle with yourself and the world. Sheep are very simple and content animals. They do not want for much. A wolf has great instinct, they are strategic, and intelligent. They have self-control and are balanced. However, they live with motives to kill anything that may cross their path. No matter what you may want or need from them, they will eventually prepare to destroy you. A dove is pure and signifies, trust, loyalty and peace.

I personally believe that we should have the spirit of all three.

With that said protect yourself, your peace, your dreams, and your time.

Progression comes with making mistakes.

Fail At Something. I Promise You Will Thank Me Later

One Sunday in church, my apostle was preaching on the subject of promotion. I don't know how everyone else perceived it, but for me, it made perfect sense. Your life cannot be promoted until you master and outperform where you are right now. This means bad attitudes, spending habits, your faith-the list goes on. We all get into situations that may bring out the worst in us. The hard part may seem to be how you are going to get out of it. However, the hard part is, fixing your mind to think positive and take the steps to fix the situation. Remember the situation I talked about in the entry before this one? How my idea was used in a similar way? When I first saw what was going on, my heart melted into pieces. I was literally sick! I told everyone who was near and dear to me in a forty-five minute time frame. The problem with that, was that I spent most of that time dwelling on what she had done instead of sitting down and doing what I was supposed to do. I don't know if you have ever seen the movie, but there is a movie about the birthing of McDonald's called, "The Founder." The owner of McDonald's; Ray Kroc, was introduced to McDonald's by the original owners. He signed on as a partner, but eventually, he took the company from them. However, in that case, they were not interested in making the company better. So, he reinvented it and made McDonald's what it is today. I said to myself, *"I would hate to be them."* Well, in that moment, that is how I felt.

I could have chosen to sit down and let my whole idea perish. I could have let the thought of someone possibly stealing it all away from me take me out. But, I didn't! I got myself together and continued to push forward. Once again, there was a valuable lesson to be learned.

I have failed a thousand times, but I made a decision to cry about it, and then, get out and figure out how to fix it.

In order to move to the next level or to a higher level in your life, you have to learn how to deal with situations. It's about God giving you opportunities to make good with, and getting a lesson and an experience out of them. The good and the bad; that is what failure and experience is all about. Learn the lessons from failure so that you don't have to repeat them.

Silence cannot be misquoted.

Embrace the Struggle

Follow your dreams. This is something you have and will hear me say constantly, because I believe that you should. Here is the gag…you still have to make money in the process. Years ago, after I released my first book, I found myself sitting in my room, staring at the wall saying, *"What do I do now?"* I had sold all of my books and put most of my profit towards bills. I wasn't working because, *I'm an artist and we don't work, we create.* Lies! All lies! If you are an artist or a person with a dream, ya better find a way to make money if you want to get the ball rolling.

I sat in that house and was so depressed! I was ashamed of getting a job, because I just wanted to act, write, and build my own. That's what people knew me as. Getting a regular nine to five would have been embarrassing. The question is, "Shanelle, how are you going to survive?" Everyone else was doing what they wanted to do every day and having a good time; at least that was what it looked like. Not me. I'm a part-time writer and a full-time employee. This was not true whatsoever. So, once again, I had to fix my mind. One day, my good girlfriend, Tiava, stopped by my house. We went on a joy ride somewhere. The next thing you know, I was bawling! I mean tears flying, mucus falling, just looking pathetic. "Tiava, I don't know what to do! Nothing is going the way that I planned. I should be on TV by now. My books should be in stores right now. I shouldn't be broke; I should have money! What happened to me? I just want to get back to being the person I used to be," I cried. Tiava is my friend for a few reasons, but one thing I love about her is, she keeps it all the way 100! She would never lie to me to make me feel good. Instead, she is going to give it to me straight with the most nonchalant look on her face and a stern, but, dry tone. She will even crack a few jokes.

She said to me, "You know what your problem is? You don't embrace the struggle." I wiped my tears and stared at her with confusion.

"Don't look at me like that," she said. "You heard what I said. You don't embrace the struggle. You can't just sit around, write books, and think about ideas. You have to put them to action and have a job to finance your life. Simple as that! People don't go from nothing to a million dollars unless they hit the lottery. Even then, you have to have money to buy the ticket."

That one conversation changed my life. No, I am not a millionaire yet, but it's closer than what I think it is. The conversation, made me realize that everything I want out of life will not just appear. I have to be proactive in every way possible to help my life to progress. A job is just like money; it is a tool. You cannot get caught up in how it makes you look. It's only temporary until you get to where you are trying to be.

I've watched my husband go through so much from high school to the present. I mean he has been through a lot! No matter how much I would complain or what we would have to go through, his favorite line was, "This is only temporary." He was right, and now we are both on a path to living out our dreams. Not embracing the struggle was the reason that I was broke for so long.

> *The struggle makes you stronger, if you can master it. .you can become successful.*

Where Are You From?

I am from West Baltimore City. I grew up in the Poplar Grove Community on the 1100 block of North Dukeland. When I wasn't there, I spent my time at my grandmother's house on Lauretta Avenue in the Edmondson Avenue Community. Just in case you are not familiar; these are a few of the roughest neighborhoods in Baltimore City. But, to me, they are home. They are low income and middle-class residences; and in most of the community. it was consistent gang violence and drug activity. My schools were not the best, either. The classrooms were freezing in the winter time as if we were sitting outside in the cold, and the text books were trash. A great number of my closest friends were either incarcerated, or lost their lives to violence. I am saying all of this to say the way I grew up was not the best, but it was definitely not the worst. My neighbors were a family, and we took care of each other. Our community raised me, along with other lifelong friends. I am not a product of my environment, but I am a product of those who took care of me. Some of my best friends are still living in those communities; young and old. They have kept me grounded over the years and have filled me with wisdom. Don't be ashamed of who you are or where you came from. That is who you are. Instead, have goals to give back to your community. Whether you live in a mansion in Beverly Hills, a shack in the country, or in a row home in Baltimore City, you are an example of what another little girl or little boy from your neighborhood could be. My city is my inspiration, because I have seen what poverty looks like first hand. My mom and dad provided for us, but there were also days when my mom had to struggle a little harder. Or my friends down the street had to come to our house when the lights were off. That inspired me to follow my dreams and focus on building a legacy that will live longer than me.

Just know that God gave you the life He gave you for a reason. It is up to you to put the puzzle together and make a beautiful portrait of it.

On the flipside of all of this is, there will be people from your environment who will try to make you feel bad for elevating and leaving. Don't let anyone make you feel bad for wanting something new. I will ever forget, back in 2009 after I lost my house and my car, I moved in with my cousin and her three kids. (That was a terrible idea, might I add. However, I learned a lot about people through that experience.) I used all of the money I had to pay for an acting class that was given by a famous actress. To some, that may sound irresponsible, but, for me, it was a calling that I had to answer; it was worth every dime. My cousin suggested that I use the money to pay a bill. Well at that time I had lost all of my bills and she lived for free so it wasn't costing me anything. I told her I really needed to be there and I could see the look on her face was about more than "giving me advice."

A few days later my aunt picked me up from the train station after my acting class. My aunt was pretty much consumed with Baltimore and everything that was going on in it. The acting coach told me I was a natural and could really go far. On the train, I decided I am moving to Los Angeles. Why not? I had no house, no car and no kids. There was nothing to hold me back. I got in the car so excited and ready to start my acting career. I told my aunt about what the acting coach said, and that I am going to save up and move to Los Angeles. She turned her face up and said, "Why do you need to move there?

You can do everything you need to do here? There is nothing in LA for you." We literally battled back in forth on this subject to the point we were both sitting in the car with attitudes. I learned three lessons from these situations. 1.) You cannot discuss all of your plans with other people, because they may try to shut it down. 2.) Never give someone the power to argue with you about *your* well-being. 3.) Always go with your gut. At the end of that weekend, that famous actress gave me her phone number and told me to give her a call whenever I needed to.

Now… this is where I say, use the resources that you have. Every few weeks I would call and have a short conversation with that actress. I begin saving up all of my money to move to Los Angeles. Finally, tax season came and I knew I would get a big refund check. I received a letter in the mail from my bank that said they had taken all of my money out of my account to pay on my car that was repossessed. Thousands of dollars! This was literally all I had to start over. I was sick to my stomach. I pulled myself together, got up, and said, *"I am going to call her and ask her if I can come out there and stay with her. I will be her assistant for free. I just needed a start."* I left the house and took a walk. Finally, I picked up the phone and called her.

"Hey, how are you doing?" I said.

"I'm good. On set at the moment, what's up?" she replied.

"Oh, that's great. Um okay… then… see you later," I said.

"Sweetie, is everything okay?"

"Yeah, I'm fine," I answered.

Then I hung up. I hung up?! What was I thinking! I'm sure she would've said yes or gave me the resources to get there. I missed out on a huge opportunity! So, back to regrets... I don't know, baby sis… that may have actually been one. After that, I never spoke to her again. When I finally called she had gotten her number changed. So… lesson four. You see an opportunity take it!

As you know, I never moved out to LA. Not because of what my aunt said; although, if I wasn't so bull headed and stubborn, her remarks could have definitely had an effect on me. I didn't move because I allowed my circumstances to keep me where I was at the moment. Which takes me to my next subject.

Money is Not an Excuse

Money should not be your reason to not go after something. If that were the case, there wouldn't be any millionaires or billionaires, because the majority of them started with nothing. I have been blessed in some crazy ways to get projects done. When I wrote my first book money just fell in my lap and instead of going shopping with all of it, I invested in my book being published. However, if that money had never come, I still would have gotten it done; it just would have taken longer than expected. If you want something bad enough, you have to be willing to invest in it, even if that means working a full-time job to pay for it. I hate to hear people say, "I can't afford it." Well, do you want to afford it? Technically I can't afford it either, but I guarantee you that if I want it bad enough, I am going to figure out how to afford it. If you ask me, you should keep that statement off of your lips and far away. Instead, you should be thinking, *"How am I going to get it?"* Where there is a will, there is a way, gorgeous!

There are six things that rich people do:

1. The rich believe in income.
2. Rich people focus on opportunities, not the obstacles they face.
3. Rich people associate with positive and successful people.
4. The rich are willing to promote themselves and their value.
5. Rich people are avid readers. (Pick up a book!)
6. Rich people grow bigger than their problems.

These references come from Youtuber Evan Carmichael. I watch his Youtube channel often, and I think you should, too.

You control your destiny. You don't need magic to do it. And, there are no magical shortcuts to solving your problems.
-Merida, Disney Movie "Brave"

The only way to get what you want in this world is through hard work.
-Tiana, The Princess and the Frog

LESSON TWELVE

Boyz to Men

This is a casual subject, but it is definitely up for discussion. Yes, we are going to discuss boys! I don't know how old you are, but I do believe that a conversation about relationships, falling in love, and all of that good stuff should be discussed before you are grown and on your own. Some parents don't want to talk about it, but in my opinion; it is setting you up for failure. It brings me peace to know that I have planted the knowledge of men and relationships into my daughters, because, then, they will not walk blindly. Hopefully, they won't fall for just anything or anybody. If they do, at least I know that I have done my part. One thing I know is, that it is inevitable… Love… One day you will fall in love with someone or want to share some kind of partnership with someone. So why not give you the advice that I have? You don't have to listen, it may not be for you, but at least you can say, "Somebody told me."

Remember when I said, *"Do you?"* This is the perfect subject to have an understanding of what that means. "*Do you,*" means focus on you and your plans. Do not...I repeat, do not compromise your plans for a guy who may be in your rearview mirror by the end of the year. We all fall crazy in love and make foolish decisions. Some we learn from, and others we fully regret. So, I will not be the one to judge you, but I will say, don't spend your teenage years and your twenties with a bird's eye view on anyone but yourself. I promise you, it will mean more in the long run. Focus on what you have going on.

He Loves Me He Loves Me Not

We will all fall in love at some point, whether it's real love or puppy love; but, when you do, don't become so consumed with being in love that you forget about you! As women/girls, we have a tendency to put so much energy into these guys. It can be so bad that we stop hanging out. No more after school activities; it's just all about him. I fell in love at a very young age. Yes, today that boy in my social studies class is my husband, but, as I said before, I forgot about ME. On top of that, this was not an easy road. I spent more time with him than I did with my friends or even with myself, and I did it for a long time. There were consistent growing pains in my relationship. Some days we were head over heels for each other, and other days we couldn't stand the sight of each other. A lot of this was because we spent way too much time together. Every day I had to see him! Everyday! When I look back now, there could have been a million things that I could have been doing.

If a person loves you, you should not have to make drastic changes in the person you are for them to love you. What I mean is, be who you are. If he wants you to change things about yourself that you love, then he should just find someone else. I mean this in the most positive way. Now, if there are negative things such as him complaining that you party more than you focus on work or school then he may have a point. It sounds like he is trying to help you. On the other hand, if he says you need to lose weight and you are already a size 4,6, or 8 he is not trying to help you, he is trying to belittle you and make you feel bad. To be honest, I don't care if you are a size 16 or 32! If you are absolutely comfortable with your weight and you are healthy, who is he to tell you to lose weight? I do believe that your health should come first; and if you need to lose weight, do it for yourself. People come in all shapes and sizes. It's how you maintain it that matters. The bottom line is, you should not have to guess if he loves you for you, or if he is feeling different *today.* That is crazy… Love me or Love me not!

> *We are not always compatible with the person we want to be with.*

Work for It

Make him work for your time. Having date nights at his house is not a date. "Netflix and Chill" is being lazy, period! Yeah, it's cool sometimes, but every date should not be in his living room in front of the television. Go out and have fun! Get to know each other. Personally, I like all types of dates, but my favorite dates are when we are doing something fun, like go kart racing, or something active. I'm a tomboy with girly girl tendencies. Of course, I love a good meal, but after a while, eating at a restaurant gets played out. Go on a day trip or do something different. If he cannot meet you beyond his or your doorstep, then shut it down and tell him, you are worth more than his mother's couch.

When my husband and I were just dating, we would take day trips to Washington, DC just to see the monuments or to New York City, just to get away. These types of relationship activities bring excitement and help to build a friendship. You may be too young to take day trips, but there are always productive things to do. Travel through your own city, grab some ice cream and take a walk. Do things that will allow you to get to know him better. Not just a movie; you can't even talk, so how will you find out who his favorite football team is?

There is nothing better than a guy who can carry on an intelligent conversation. It takes time to get to know a person. This is where courting comes in. Most of my young teenage readers should not be courted at a young age, but you should still know what it means. Courting is when a guy is pursuing you to possibly be his wife. Rarely do you hear the word anymore. The reason is, because women do not demand to be courted as we used to. Which, in my opinion, is a problem that we need to work on. We settle for less, because we are not showing our value or that we have interest in being married. I didn't understand, nor did

I think about courting until I was ready to be married. I gave myself away at a young age without that thought in mind. Setting your standards is preparation to you being treated as expected. If you are under the age of eighteen and have been permitted by your parents to date, you should still treat dating as if you are being courted, and so should he. With that said, I am not saying that every woman should aspire to be married. That is totally your business, but if you are dating, you should aspire to be respected and treated as the queen you are.

Guys take advantage of what comes easy to them. I don't care who you are. You're treated the way you portray yourself to be. If you act like a "thot", easy or sleazy, you will be treated that way, period. The moment that a man knows you are easily attainable, he may switch up. This is where the cat and mouse games come in, and most of the time, the guy is both. In the beginning he will put in all the effort that he can to get your attention, but the moment that he gets you, it's a wrap. Now, you are hooked and he is missing in action. While you are busy chasing him down, he is doing his best to be unavailable. You have to do the same! You do not need to be available every time he calls. Make him wait and wonder. I am not saying to not show him that you like him or to play games. But, hey, sometimes you have to make them miss you. You should still be pleasant, but don't spend your whole day calling to find out what he is doing. Give him a chance to miss you and call you.

Believe It or Be Played

When I say I have had my share of naive moments. I have stuck by people in the past even when they have clearly showed me who they are. Guilty as charged! So, take it from me. When a guy shows you or tell you that he is not good for you, believe him! Don't run back trying to make it work, just believe him. I promise you, it is not worth the stress and time you will waste trying to make it work. Better yet, if his family tells you he is not right, believe them! Most of the time they are right.

This is where the problem comes in. You have to do your best to identify if these people are giving you good or bad information. So, play it cool until the character you've heard about shows up. When he shows up, run for your life!

This is not a suggestion that people do not change; however, you have to be the judge of that. You can give him another chance; just don't keep playing the fool. Again, I am speaking from experience.

During my twenties, my boyfriend and I had a long break up. I dated a little here and there. There was this one guy whom I really liked. He was like the neighborhood star in a sense. He knew people in high places and was in college playing basketball. I cannot say that is why I liked him honestly; I think it was his long braids that I fell for. (I'm laughing way too hard!) But, he was sort of a manipulative, self-absorbed, arrogant jerk. He thought he was God's gift to the world! But, because so many girls wanted him and he looked like he had a bright future, I gave him a pass. Wrong move! At the end of the day, he was still a jerk and he didn't want what I wanted at the time. I was just too boy crazy and blind to see that he was wasting my time. On top of that, he wasn't very nice. The day that I finally walked away from that entire situation was like a breath of fresh air. What I learned from him was that no matter who a person is, they are never too good to treat you well. Don't get blinded by the hype.

Sex… The Touchy Subject

Now this is a very touchy subject, but I'm going to go there anyway, because if no one else has told you then you've heard it first hand from me. This is the topic where most parents cringe while talking to their teenage daughters. But, these days "the talk" comes a little earlier. I would rather my child get the real from me then in school from an un experienced knuckle head or a girlfriend who doesn't know any better. Even worse, television and social media. Hearing someone say "I love you" does not mean you have to give up the goods. You know the goods. My mother used to call it, "my goodies". Those are your goodies, and I promise you there is so much value in it. Girl, it is powerful, l and the longer you keep it the more value it has. Sex is not all it's cut out to be until you have a real chemistry with a person. I am not saying you don't have feelings or understand what love is, I am saying that until you become aware of who you are as a young woman and your value to this world, you will not have a true understanding of your chemistry with a person. Besides, the words, "I love you," are used so loosely. Now, if you make the decision to have sex, just know that it's not something that you can take back. Make sure it's with someone that you can absolutely trust, and that he is a friend, and you are protected. PLEASE DO NOT TELL YOUR PARENTS THAT SHANELLE SAID, "I CAN HAVE SEX, BUT." And add your own little philosophy there.

I just know that at the end of the day, you have your own mind. As your big sister in a book, I can only relay this message to you. Right now, just have fun; and if he doesn't understand when you say, "the goodies are off limits," then he can move to the next. "Bye Felicia!" as Ice Cube would say.

I am sure you are becoming curious as your body is changing and temptation is flowing, but I cannot stress it enough that it's so much more exciting as an adult when you both know what you are doing, who you are, and what you want. I believe in soul ties. Soul ties is the physical act of giving yourself to another person that makes you vulnerable to such a connection. Sexual intercourse is supposed to be used to unify two people in a way that is nurturing and empowering. In my eyes this can be a good and bad thing, because it gives the other person full access to you and you to them. You can transfer a person's good and bad ways unto your being. I also believe that sex can cloud your mind and your judgment about someone. There are a lot of women in this world who have fallen for the wrong guy, but because of their sexual relationship, they allowed things to go on that should not have taken place. They have been manipulated and made bad decisions.

After my first child, my husband and I (who was my boyfriend at the time) broke up. At that time, I felt unappreciated, confused, lost, not pretty, unorganized, the list goes on! I decided to practice celibacy. It wasn't difficult for me in the beginning, because my focus was on my daughter and getting us into a better situation. After a while it got a little difficult, but I began to focus on becoming closer to God and my future goals. As time went on, I had a flow going and I had a clear mind. I honestly felt like a weight was lifted off of my shoulders.

Sometimes, not all of the time, but sometimes a relationship can drain you and cause you to lose focus.

Meeting the Family

First of all, every guy that you date should not meet your parents unless you are under the age of eighteen. In this case, yes, you are a minor and your family needs to know the kind of company you are keeping. If you are ashamed to bring them home, then they should probably not be in your space. That is just my opinion. If you are over eighteen, you should be very selective of who is at a standard to meet your parents. When I say that, I mean, have enough respect for your parents to know that this guy is a keeper. He is respectful and we have been dating long enough for me to feel him out. Don't just bring every guy you meet up in your parent's house! Your family will look at you like you are half crazy. Hold your family at a standard that says, "I respect you enough to not just bring random guys around you." You may not always agree with their opinions of a guy, but at least hear what they have to say. Your family's home should be a sacred place so be careful of the energy you allow into it.

Personally, I find value in my parents' opinion. They may not always be right, but the advice that is received goes a long way. Furthermore, it shows that guy that you have a family that has your back. That is important, because he knows that he is up against a girl with a family that doesn't play.

Girl Code 101

Never, I repeat NEVER hook up with your ex-boyfriend's friends or relatives. You will never hear the end of it! Especially, if you two get back together. Secondly, they are going to talk about you and compare their experiences with you. Whatever that experience may have been. Yes, guys gossip just like girls. You will be the hot topic of the conversation. How awkward would it be to run into your ex and his friend at the same time knowing that you dated both of them? I'm just saying.

Remember when I said stop telling your friends all of your business? Girl! I meant that. They don't have to know every little detail. Keep something for yourself. You never know if they are taking inventory of all of your little secrets, or if they are intrigued by your new love situation and want to get to know him for her self. Yes, it happens all of the time. Better yet, there are those who get jealous that you have a new situation going on. None of these may be true in your case. Just be mindful of the amount of beans you spill.

After a Break Up

The worst thing to do after a break up is to sit around crying and reminiscing on your past. Yes, you should give yourself some time to cry it out and get over the bumps and bruises, but after a week or so get yourself together. Get cute, hang out with friends, enjoy YOU! Don't jump right back into dating so fast. Take time to figure yourself out and love up on *you!*

I don't want to sound like I am not compassionate, because that is not the case. I've been there. I've been through all of the emotions, but who wants to stay in that dark place forever. You still have a life to live. Learn from it and move on. If there is a possibility of reconnection, I suggest you give it some time before establishing yourself as a couple again. Start over as friends, have fun and don't do anything that will cause mixed signals until you are absolutely ready to jump back in. Reasons for breaking up are always a factor that should be considered. The conversation should take place if it has not been resolved. If he was abusive in anyway or consistent with cheating, run for the hills. Bye, boo! More than likely, these things will not change, or it will be ages before they do. You have to make it clear that you will not tolerate certain behavior. If he has no interest in becoming a better person and shows no value in the relationship, I suggest you two see where his life goes without you in the picture. If he starts to do things to better him self, it may be worth the while; but, again, this is excluding abuse. Nah, we're not having it, homie.

They Get Jealous Too!

Just because he is your boyfriend does not mean that he will always be supportive. There are guys out here that can bare a little jealousy and may even be intimidated by a woman. Once again, you should not dim your light for him, either. Continue to become your best you. He will either do his part or he will not. It is not your job to make him feel like a man. I say this, because there are cases when the woman makes more money, is more responsible, or has more confidence. In order to make her man feel better about who he is, she may stop shopping as much or stop traveling and buying nice things. All, because he can't afford it? How unfair is that? Why should you have to leave below your standards to make him feel better? How about he gets on your level. If you are on a great career path and are knocking down your goals why can't he do the same? It may be a little different from your path, but if he is making a way, that is what is important. It is not your fault if he doesn't feel adequate or live up to your potential. You should be an inspiration just as he should be an inspiration to you.

Support each other. If he is struggling with achieving a goal, there is nothing wrong with you assisting him if he is not too prideful to allow you to. We have to pull each other up, but it is not your job to carry all of the weight. "You cannot have the "I have to do for him, if he can't do for him" mentality. Girl, you are not his mother! So, do not get caught up in doing motherly duties.

He can smell your weakness. If you do everything under the sun for him, he will always expect you to. He will know how to control you with his emotions. Please do not allow this to happen. We can get so caught up in loving someone that we don't realize that they are using our love against us. There is a young man that tells his girlfriend that he is going to kill himself. First of all, this is scary, don't sit around waiting for him to do it; get away and send him some help. He would go through these little fits and charades and depressions whenever he wanted her to stay with him. He uses pity to keep her around. This is insane, but it happens and once again if you are blind, you will not see.

Move in For What?

Okay, so after being on my own for a few months, my boyfriend moved in. For so many reasons, I do not recommend this. Number one…the moment he moves in with you, you will lose a few things. One of those things is privacy. He is always there, it's no longer your space; it's *our* space. You now have to consider him in every decision in the house. For example, I had a bright red sofa, beautiful magenta pink drapes and a multi colored chandelier. Not to mention the canvases of Marilyn

Monroe and Aubrey Hepburn. It was a home fit for a young queen. Nothing there said King. Was I willing to compromise? No, I wasn't! Sorry, I was young and unwed. Besides, he moved into *my* bachelorette pad. Number two…you will become a house wife early. Cooking dinner for him and washing his laundry. It's nothing wrong with cooking for a man, but when you are young, you should not be cooking for a man every night. Sure, he can come over for dinner, but when you two live together, you have definitely taken on the role as a house- wife. Number three… It is very true that you never know a person until you move in with them. If they are junky or don't clean or work on all of your pet peeves; you are not in a situation to simply deal with it.

One day I was in the salon and heard a young lady talking about her and her boyfriend. She was just going on and on about her relationship. In my mind, I was telling her, "Shut up, you're talking too much!" But, what caught my ear was her talking about how they would be moving in together after she graduates high school. Eighteen years old and she had it all mapped out. I've been there, so I get it. You want to be so grown so fast. During my time there, I watched her boyfriend drop her off and pick her up in her car! Yes, my boyfriend drove my car, too, so I know the game. I asked her if he had a job. She said no. "Does he go to school?" Her answer was no. So, my first thought was, *"Well why does he need your car and why doesn't he have his own?"* It's not a thing of being judgmental, but I have learned that if a guy is not willing to get out here and do his own thing, then he will continue to do what he is doing for as long as you allow it. He will empty your gas tank and get money from you to fill it up. You cannot expect someone to do better if you settle for less. If he is not showing any potential or trying to excel, then you need to elevate yourself and tell him to holler at you when he gets himself together. Life is too short for the foolishness. We have all, including myself, wasted our precious time trying to push someone who is not ready to move. "No love lost and no hard feelings, but this energy is not good for me." This stands for friends, family, whoever.

Sometimes we can get consumed with our relationships to a point where it is detrimental to our health. I know a woman that spent most of her time obsessed over her boyfriend, his cheating habits, and how he treated her. Every conversation was about the other woman and his family. How he did her and how angry she was. She literally ended up in the hospital, because of the consumption of negativity she took in over this man. It was hard to listen to. Love should not be painful. Again, we all go through our stuff. I have been through my own share of "sick in love" moments, but never to the point where my health was involved. When you feel yourself getting to the point of no return, like psycho killer crazy or obsessed, that means it's time to bare back and take several seats. Don't put your health or freedom in danger, because of love. It is not worth your time, energy or the bail money you will need to get out of jail.

50/ 50

Nah, relationships are 100%/100%. You give, I give. Period. Like I said before, you should not empty your pockets, your energy, or your soul for anyone. Especially, if he has a track record of not reciprocating. Taking on another person's baggage can be exhausting. No friendship or fun in a relationship can be exhausting. Being with someone who constantly depends on you can be exhausting. It's all soul crushing and exhausting! You can't change a person who doesn't want to change. As women have a tendency of thinking we can change men. We can't! There is no secret formula called "Jerk Be Gone." If he is a jerk, he will be a jerk until he is ready to make a change. You are going to stress yourself out trying to change dude. Just stop and move on. You're still young; if it is meant to be, it will be. Remember, time does not wait for you. Before you know it, you will look back and say, "I've spent two years trying to change this fool." Nah sis, move on.

In conclusion to this short and sweet topic, I will say again TAKE CARE OF YOURSELF, FIRST. Men/boys will forever be around. Trust me when I say, you will need all of your energy, so put yourself first, and love yourself first. You cannot love anyone until you love yourself. One day your heart will be broken. I know it sounds cold, but, it's true; and it may be more than once. Honey, it is not the end of the world. I have a friend who is a few years younger than me. All I ever hear her talk about is being lonely and wanting a man. She had been in a relationship for ten years of her life, very similar to me. Now, they are broken up and she spends a lot of her daily conversations talking about wanting children and a man. She is still in her twenties. My advice to her was to spend this time living her best life and learning more about her self. This is not a time to mope around wishing you were tied down! You better "Netflix and Chill" by yourself, take a trip, something! Take advantage of where you are before you have to consider someone else's feelings. If you have your own apartment, decorate it to your liking. Make it feel just like you. Be the bachelorette that your "Boo'd up" friends envy!

He Did What?!

This is a very serious topic. I contemplated on writing about this topic, because it is a touchy subject as well. So, earlier, I talked about how a guy can be jealous. Jealousy can turn into being possessive or obsessive. When a man feels that you are his possession he believes that he can handle you however he pleases. What you do not stand for is abuse - mentally or physically. If a person can say they love you, and physically or mentally abuse you at the same time- that, my love, is not love. Regardless of how he dresses it up. There are enough men in this world for you to wait on the right one. There are ways to tell if a guy is possessive or obsessive: 1) If he doesn't want you to give your time to anyone else. 2) If he watches your every move. 3) If he tries to change the way you look or gets jealous when other friends come around. 4) If the smallest topic or situation makes him angry. I'm sure there are a lot more. Just don't fall for a cute smile; we all have layers. When you are falling for someone, you have to get to the deep-rooted parts that he may try to hide. Then you will know what you are dealing with.

The bottom line is, this is not a love song or a romantic comedy. I am not saying that love is not an overwhelmingly amazing part of life, I am just saying that it is not always peaches and cream. Love shows up through the rough times, not just chocolate and cards. Is this person willing to ride through the storms with you or is he just around to ride the wave? Nothing is more important than that in my eyes. One more thing, don't underestimate the power of love and what it can make you do. Be smart and stay away from your crazy. Yes, I said, YOUR CRAZY. I don't care if you are fifteen or twenty-one. We all have an ounce of crazy that we need to keep under control. Do not embarrass yourself or devalue yourself just because someone has done something to hurt your feelings. It is not worth what could possibly become permanent damage to you or them either physical or mental. I hope you have received something from this lesson. I wish I had a better understanding of love and the opposite sex as a young woman. Please don't take it lightly.

Your Boyfriend has a Monthly Cycle

Guys have a monthly cycle just like we do. I can literally feel the change of energy in the air when my husband is going through "PMS." It's funny, but it's true. His whole attitude is "IRKY". Like, "Chill out, bro. It's not that serious! He gets very irritable and every answer is short and nonchalant. That is my cue to get dressed, get cute, and get out of dodge! I don't have time for your changes and mine too; it is just too much, boo. It's just too much…

Deal Breakers

My deal breakers and your deal breakers may be different, but please don't take these with a grain a salt. Remember that if you allow a person to start a cycle, they will continue it until you are broken.

1. Don't touch my coins! – It is and will never be okay for a man or anyone who loves you to steal from you. It is hurtful and it will haunt you throughout the relationship. Every time money looks short you will look at him as being the culprit. The trust will be gone out the window along with his bags.

2. Getting involved with someone close to you. Don't get me wrong. If we are exclusive, then cheating is a no no period. But if he tries someone in your circle, that is a major deal breaker- how about this "Don't humiliate me, period!"

3. Suga Momma!- You're paying your bills and his. No! He needs to make his on way the same way you have to. No job, no car, no house, no dreams, bad credit and could care less about making it better. You are always taking HIM out on a date and upgrading his life? He is not potential, he is a mess! There is nothing wrong with helping someone out EVERY ONCE IN AWHILE, but if you are sponsoring his every move and you have been for some time. That is a problem! Let him go back to his mother and you get back to being single, sexy and free!

4. The disrespect! – I'm sure we may have covered this and a few others. However, you know how you should be handled and spoken to. There is no reason for me to go into detail. If this is ongoing and you have already set your expectations… - Bye!

5. Baggage- We all have baggage, but when you become a victim of your baggage that becomes a problem. Constantly, whining about why you cannot do something; so much is holding you back… That energy is draining! Get out here and figure out how to get it! But if he is allowing his baggage to keep the both of you down; he has to go!

6. Anger – I spoke on this before as well, but if he cannot control his anger and it turns physical that is a problem. When I say "physical" I mean just that whether it's against you or your walls- "Nope, homie I worked too hard for nice things and you WILL NOT DESTROY THEM!" He needs to seek counseling sis.

Do's and Don'ts

Your turn! There are some do's and don'ts for you as well, because of course, WE are never wrong!

Do's

1. Respect him the same way you want him to respect you. You can't demand to be treated like a queen and you don't treat him like a king.

2. Listen and let him talk. You cannot hear if you are both screaming. Listen with your eyes and your ears, show him that you are considering his point of view

3. Make him feel special sometimes. We like to go on dates and get gifts. It's okay to buy your man a gift or take him out for dinner, just to say "I see your effort and I appreciate it."

4. Speak life into him! I can see the weight of the world on my husband's shoulders sometimes and there have been days that I have made it worst. We have to keep the men in our lives uplifted so that they know they are not alone and that they are doing a great job. This is vital, because for some men they have never heard theses words "You are doing such a great job and I am very proud of you!" -But only say it if you mean it and if he deserves it!

5. Make him remember why YOU ARE THE ONE. Yes, he should see you at your best and at your worst, but not ALWAYS at your worst!

6. Find interest in the things he loves as well. If he loves sports get involved a little, but don't get

pushy or try to force him to involve you. Just show that you have interest in the things that he loves.

7. Consider that there may be other women in his life such as his mother and/or sisters. You may want to be all of the woman he needs, but bottom line is they are a part of his life too so don't be selfish.

8. Last, but not least! His deal breakers are the same for you.

Don'ts

1. Don't ever try to play him against his mother. You will never win. Men love their mothers. For the most part she can do NO WRONG, but if you feel disrespected in anyway, I suggest that you let him know. If he doesn't take care of it then you speak directly to her, woman to woman. Try to keep your cool. On another note, if she seems cool, build a good relationship with her. But never forget she is still HIS mother.

2. Don't belittle him. Words can cut like a knife. I know because I have a razor tongue myself. It

took years for me to learn how to control it. The things that you say will carry with him, even when you think it's over.

3. Keep some things just between you two. The moment that you begin to let everyone into your relationship they will take that as an opportunity to always have an opinion and sometimes we only tell our side and it makes him look like the bad guy. (And you know you started it!) If the relationship is worth saving; learn how to sit down and communicate with each other. This is a habit that should be exercised often.

4. Stop being a nag! Every little thing is not a big deal. Believe me I am speaking on all of my experiences. Don't turn into your mother!

5. You are not his mother so stop trying to be. You cannot control his every move! You are going to end up in a hospital with padded rooms and stray jackets! Chill! If he is being a dog, then let him walk himself right up out of your life. Don't stress yourself about what he may or may not be doing. Your tuition is strong enough and the alarms will start going off. When they do,

handle them accordingly. FYI: Stop stalking his social media your wasting your valuable time. Go build an empire or something!

6. Don't play the blame game. He is not always in the wrong. Check yourself and be woman enough to say "You know what, I was wrong. My apologies"

7. Stop being so insecure! This rolls into number five. Girl fix your crown and wipe those insecurities off of your face. If he forgot who you are, show him! Remember, success is the best revenge and put on your favorite lipstick while doing it!

8. Last but not least DON'T BE A FOOL! Take that how you want to. You're a smart girl, you will figure it out.

What are deal breakers for you in a relationship?

Remember, if you don't respect yourself you cannot expect someone else to respect you. The way you treat a person in the beginning may be the foundation to how your relationship will go. Vice versa, the way that you allow someone to treat you will be the foundation that you lay for them. List five of your deal breakers and stick to them as you journey into the world of dating. If you want to write more, feel free. If you don't stick to them, you are giving a person permission to handle you however they please.

1. ______________________________

2. ______________________________

3. ______________________________

4. ______________________________

5. ______________________________

What do you value in a relationship?

____

____

____

____

____

Remember, what you saw as a child growing up does not have to be your example of what a "good relationship" looks like. It may not be as perfect as your parents or as imperfect. Write your own story and try to stay away from "generational curses", break the cycle. You deserve to be loved!

"You've got to learn to leave the table when love is no longer being served."

-Nina Simone

"Love is louder than the pressure to be perfect."

-Demi Lovato

"If you are lucky enough to be different, don't you ever change."

-Taylor Swift

"I am not just a pop star, I am not just my outfits. I am not just my anxious, anxiety written, depressed self. I am you."

-Lady Gaga

LESSON THIRTEEN

A Letter to My Younger Self

All of the lessons that I am laying on you would also be to my younger self. If I could talk to that girl at fifteen, or eighteen, twenty-one, or even twenty- five; it would be something like this:

Dear Shanelle,

I know life has not always been pretty and life will continue to throw you lemons. Just push through and learn from them. Please know that you will be okay and it is okay to be you. Don't put so much energy in negative people. You cannot change them, you can only change the way you see them. Stop spending so much time trying to figure out how people feel about you. It will stunt your growth and curve your focus. Besides, their feelings have nothing to do with you. Shanelle, it's okay to ask for help; it doesn't make you less of a person. You are amazing and full of talent. Don't waste it!

Get out there and explore life! Stop trying to be grown so fast! You have the rest of your life to do that. Those bills can wait, and so can living with your boyfriend. Stop worrying about Anthony and explore life; he will be there, I promise. Build and hone your craft. Put every awaken moment into becoming the best you. Take New York by storm! Study to be the actress you've always dreamed of becoming. Don't bend your values or your plans for anyone. Jump out there and go get what you want with no hesitation. Save, save, save your money and invest into something you love. Don't be scared! Your family will be okay, but they need you to be their rock and lead them out. One day, your mom and dad may not be here, so, listen to the advice they give you. Indulge in to every moment that will birth a great memory. Going to work for pennies is not more important than the time spent with your family. Spend more time with friends and building relationships. Don't be such a loner! People look up to you, so be mindful of what you do. There will be two beautiful little girls who love you unconditionally. They will look up to you, so give them a reason to. Make mistakes and stop thinking so far in the future, because you only have right now! Stay out of your head, you think too much! What are you going to do right now to make your future brighter? Everything will be okay, just stay true to who you are and put God first. One more thing, I know you think you are superwoman, but you cannot do a million things at one time. It will get you nowhere. Master one thing at a time. Focus, girl, focus. Don't be afraid to live out loud with great intention… You ready? Let's go!

Love Always and Forever,

YOU

Life is full of ups and downs. It will never be easy. My father asked me one day, "What are ya'll going to do when I die?" My smart sarcastic mouth thought, *"Live…"* Without realizing how drastically life would change when it actually happened. Don't take life for granted. Every day that you wake up, give thanks. Be grateful for the things that we take advantage of. God gave you eyes to see, a voice to speak, legs to walk, and so much more. Someone didn't receive all of that or lost theirs. Can you only imagine? Imagine waking up one day and not being able to see. That has to be one of the scariest feelings in the world. So, thank God for that. I used to complain a lot. I would wake up mad, complaining about my job, not having money, or whatever I felt was not working in my favor. It felt like a dark cloud was over me. That is not the way to be. Start by being thankful for what you do have. That way, you will diminish that negative energy. Recently, I woke up in such a funky mood. I was exuding negativity. My mind was filled with writing this book, finishing a script, moving, my girls and whatever else popped up in my brain. I complained about not being where I want to be, and finally, my Anthony told me to man up! How rude! I'm telling him about all of my issues and he says, "man up." Well, I deserved it, because instead of working through my circumstances and getting it done, I focused on all the bad things. Instead of putting flexibility in my schedule, I had to stick to it or it would fall apart. Well, that was a part of my problem right there. There was no way that I could always stick to my schedule, because it changes from day to day. Bottom line is, life is not always filled with a to-do list. Some days you will have to go with the flow and just relax. Don't lose sight of your focus, but don't lose sight of what's important, either, and that's living.

I pray that you take life by the horns and hold on tight. Do not waste time, for it is the most valuable asset in your life. Once it is gone, you will never get it back. Do what you love and be grateful for what you have; that is the only way to acquire more. I know some of you may say I'm lecturing (laughing), but it means more to me that you are living your best life, than allowing it to slip away.

Below, you will find diary entries from my own personal diaries. I want you to see that I am no different from you. I go through the same things that you go through and so does your favorite celebrity. Just continue to be who you are and enhance that part of you through your journey of womanhood.

I pray that this book will be a tool for you, and that it changes your outlook on life. Girl, it's only life; don't take everything so serious! I love you, Queen! Peace.

Your Big Sister in a Book,

Shanelle Sara'Nita

My Diary

This diary entry is from October 10, 2009 1:45pm. This was a time in my life when I was very lost and unhappy. I had no idea where I was supposed to be and I couldn't settle myself long enough to figure it out. I had recently lost everything I owned. This was the start of finding myself.

Dear Diary,

Today is one of those days. I am blessed and grateful to be alive, though I feel very closed in and dried up. I'm at Anthony's house even though I feel like he is the only one who wants me here. I am very uncomfortable and I need to just go home. I would like to get back into my own place. I miss having my own. Some days I try so hard to be grateful for what I do have and not what I don't, but it's really hard. I know God will bless me very soon with fulfilling my dreams. I'll probably be a late bloomer, but that's okay. As long as my closest family members are there to celebrate with me. One thing that I do know is that this struggle has made me a better person. I used to be so arrogant and I took advantage of the little power I did have... Well, you reap what you sow, but I am growing and maturing every single day. Things will change, I'm sure of it. I have also looked down on some people in the past. Being able to admit these things have shown me my growth and that I am becoming a better person. Lately, I've been thinking about death and getting older. What do I want to leave behind when I am gone? Maybe that is why I have been feeling so anxious, because I don't want to spend so much more of my life living this way. I see great things in our (family) future. I would like to start fresh and not dwell on the past.

Love Always,

Shanelle S. Ladd

You know what's funny? This was so many years ago and I signed my name as Shanelle S. Ladd. My maiden name is Shanelle S. Williams. So, I guess I manifest my marriage into existence. So, I guess I will start to write billionaire on everything!

I don't know when this next entry was written, but I am sure it was in fall of 2009. This was right before my move to New York. I finally had something to look forward to.

Dear Diary,

Sometimes I wake up down and discouraged. Somedays I wake up with a sense of hope and happiness. Knowing that I am going to make it to the top soon. Sometimes I am even scared of my future and what it may hold. But, you know what? I know that God not only has something, but a lot in store for me. Lately, I've been worrying that Anthony and I won't make it, but he reassures me that we are going to make it together. I love him and I have faith and trust him. It's going to be hard, yes! God will see us through it all. I believe that we will be okay. I mean, who would I really want to celebrate life with, besides him and my family. Everybody else, I will see you when I see you. Well, next week I will be leaving for NYC. I'm staying with my aunt Shawn. I have three hundred dollars to my name, but I'm not trippin.' I will make a way. The next few years will be hard, but I'm sure we will be okay. Anthony plans to go to the Navy. I hope and pray that he does. He will as long as he focuses and doesn't procrastinate. Even though we are struggling, I'm happy. I guess it's because I am finally moving to New York. This has been my dream since I was in the fourth grade. It was also to be on a billboard in Times Square and live with my best friend. We are no longer friends so that's dead, but the billboard thing. I'm still working on it.

See you in the stars,

Shanelle

Sept. 1, 2014

Dear Diary,

I'm listening to Pandora and I felt the need to write. I'm so grateful for life! Even with all its trials and tribulations. God is so awesome. His love is completely overwhelming at times. I am finally producing my own work and I am so thankful. My book dropped last year and my play, "Our family Secrets" had a private viewing yesterday and will be premiering next week. Chloe'Rae is so beautiful and healthy. I couldn't ask for a better daughter. Anthony and I are trying to make it, but some days he gets on my last nerves. Some days I just want to quit, but I often pray for change and a closer, more loving and trustworthy relationship. We have been through so much. My car is broken, bills are past due, but God is still God! It's going to be okay. I'm trying to become a lot more disciplined in all aspects of my life. Especially with my money and health. Just living better. I have a trainer now. He believes in me being fit and being a better person. I just have to believe in myself and discipline my habits, good and bad. Some days, I'm down and I break, but I'm so excited about my show. I can't believe I am finally putting up my own work. I have the most amazing group of actors. They have been so supportive through this entire experience. Simply thankful. Simply blessed. Simply me.

These are just a few of my private conversations with myself and my journal. There are tons more of course, but some were too private to share. Keeping a journal of my life has helped me to evaluate my growth. Sometimes I look back to see what I was going through at that time and if it is something has not been addressed. Use your journal to be your therapy and your guide. Use it to evaluate your path and where you have been. I hope it has been some help to you.

www.ingramcontent.com/pod-product-compliance
Lightning Source LLC
LaVergne TN
LVHW050614100826
845148LV00011B/1582

* 9 7 8 0 5 7 8 6 6 2 6 6 4 *